MW01485002

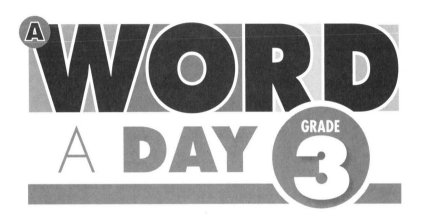

A WORD A DAY GRADE 3

Editorial Development: Marilyn Evans
Robyn Raymer
Sarita Chávez
Silverman
Susan Rose Simms
Copy Editing: Carrie Gwynne
Art Direction: Cheryl Puckett
Cover Design: David Price
Design/Production: Susan Bigger
John D. Williams

EMC 2793

Evan-Moor
EDUCATIONAL PUBLISHERS®
Helping Children Learn since 1979

Congratulations on your purchase of some of the finest teaching materials in the world.

Correlated
to State Standards

CPSIA: Printed by McNaughton & Gunn, Saline, MI USA. [4/2011]

Weekly Walk-Through

Each week of **A Word a Day** follows the same format,
making it easy for both students and teacher to use.

Words of the Week

Four new words are presented each week. A definition, example sentence, and discussion prompts are provided for each word.

Part of Speech The part of speech is identified. You may or may not want to share this information with the class, depending on the skill level of your students.

Example Sentence Each new word is used in a sentence designed to provide enough context for students to easily grasp its meaning. The same sentence is found in the reproducible student dictionary, which begins on page 148.

Critical Attributes Prompt Discussion questions are provided that require students to identify features that are and are not attributes of the target word. This is one of the most effective ways to help students recognize subtleties of meaning.

Definition Each word is defined in a complete sentence. The same definition is found in the reproducible student dictionary, which begins on page 148.

Week 1
A Word a Day

impatient
adjective
An **impatient** person is always in a hurry and finds it hard to wait.

The **impatient** man left the bank because the line was too long.

Which of these show **impatient** behavior?
• a toddler screaming for the toy that fell out of her stroller
• a teenager waiting politely until everyone finishes dinner
• a child waiting quietly in line to buy ice cream in a crowded store
• a girl calling for help while the teacher is with someone else
• a boy pulling on his mother's sleeve while she's on the phone

What makes you **impatient**? What can you do to make it easier to wait?

appliance
noun
An **appliance** is a household machine that is used for a special purpose.

Our toaster is the oldest **appliance** in our kitchen. The microwave is the newest.

Which of these are household **appliances**?
• a pillow
• a blender
• a doorknob
• a refrigerator
• a vacuum cleaner

Which **appliance** do you use most often at home? What do you use it for?

Week 1
A Word a Day

appropriate
adjective
When something is **appropriate**, it is right for that situation.

It's **appropriate** to wear nice clothing to a wedding.

Which of the following activities are **appropriate**?
• throwing food on the floor
• saying "thank you" after receiving a gift
• taking your friend's toy without asking
• wearing a bathing suit to the swimming pool
• raising your hand in school when you have a question

What is the **appropriate** way to behave at an orchestra concert? How about at a football game?

mumble
verb
When you **mumble**, you don't speak clearly.

After the dentist numbed her mouth, Ariana could only **mumble**.

Which words mean about the same as **mumble**?
• yell
• mutter
• declare
• murmur
• grumble

What would you say to someone who **mumbles** in order to get him or her to speak more clearly?

Personal Connection Prompt Students are asked to share an opinion, an idea, or a personal experience that demonstrates their understanding of the new word.

How to Present the Words

Use one of the following methods to present each word:

• Write the word on the board. Then read the definition and the example sentence, explaining as needed before conducting oral activities.

• Make an overhead transparency of the lesson page that shows the word. Then guide students through the definition, example sentence, and oral activities.

• Reproduce the dictionary on pages 148–159 for each student, or provide each student with a student practice book. (See inside front cover.) Have students find the word in their dictionaries, and then guide them through the definition, example sentence, and oral activities.

End-of-Week Review

Review the four words of the week through oral and written activities designed to reinforce student understanding.

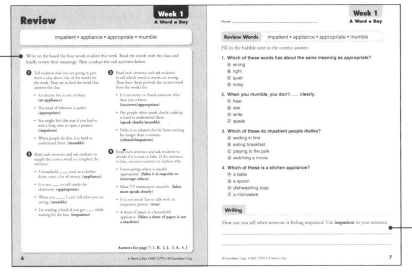

Oral Review

Four oral activities provide you with prompts to review the week's words.

Written Assessment

A student reproducible containing four multiple-choice items and an open-ended writing activity can be used to assess students' mastery.

Additional Features

- Reproducible student dictionary

- Cumulative word index

impatient

adjective

An **impatient** person is always in a hurry and finds it hard to wait.

The **impatient** man left the bank because the line was too long.

Which of these show **impatient** behavior?

- a toddler screaming for the toy that fell out of her stroller
- a teenager waiting politely until everyone finishes dinner
- a child waiting quietly in line to buy ice cream in a crowded store
- a girl calling for help while the teacher is with someone else
- a boy pulling on his mother's sleeve while she's on the phone

What makes you **impatient**? What can you do to make it easier to wait?

appliance

noun

An **appliance** is a household machine that is used for a special purpose.

Our toaster is the oldest **appliance** in our kitchen. The microwave is the newest.

Which of these are household **appliances**?

- a pillow
- a blender
- a doorknob
- a refrigerator
- a vacuum cleaner

Which **appliance** do you use most often at home? What do you use it for?

A Word a Day • EMC 2793 • © Evan-Moor Corp.

appropriate

adjective

When something is **appropriate**, it is right for that situation.

It's **appropriate** to wear nice clothing to a wedding.

Which of the following activities are **appropriate**?

- throwing food on the floor
- saying "thank you" after receiving a gift
- taking your friend's toy without asking
- wearing a bathing suit to the swimming pool
- raising your hand in school when you have a question

What is the **appropriate** way to behave at an orchestra concert? How about at a football game?

mumble

verb

When you **mumble**, you don't speak clearly.

After the dentist numbed her mouth, Ariana could only **mumble**.

Which words mean about the same as **mumble**?

- yell
- mutter
- declare
- murmur
- grumble

What would you say to someone who **mumbles** in order to get him or her to speak more clearly?

Review

impatient • appliance • appropriate • mumble

Write on the board the four words studied this week. Read the words with the class and briefly review their meanings. Then conduct the oral activities below.

1 Tell students that you are going to give them a clue about one of the words for the week. They are to find the word that answers the clue.

- An electric fan is one of these. **(an appliance)**

- This kind of behavior is polite. **(appropriate)**

- You might feel this way if you had to wait a long time to open a present. **(impatient)**

- When people do this, it is hard to understand them. **(mumble)**

2 Read each sentence and ask students to supply the correct word to complete the sentence.

- A household ____, such as a clothes dryer, costs a lot of money. **(appliance)**

- It is not ____ to yell inside the classroom. **(appropriate)**

- When you ____, I can't tell what you are saying. **(mumble)**

- Try reading a book if you get ____ while waiting for the bus. **(impatient)**

3 Read each sentence and ask students to tell which word or words are wrong. Then have them provide the correct word from the week's list.

- It is incorrect to thank someone who does you a favor. **(incorrect/appropriate)**

- Shy people often speak clearly, making it hard to understand them. **(speak clearly/mumble)**

- Pablo is so relaxed that he hates waiting for longer than a minute. **(relaxed/impatient)**

4 Read each sentence and ask students to decide if it is true or false. If the sentence is false, instruct students to explain why.

- Interrupting others is usually appropriate. **(false; it is impolite to interrupt others)**

- Most TV newscasters mumble. **(false; most speak clearly)**

- It is not much fun to talk with an impatient person. **(true)**

- A sheet of paper is a household appliance. **(false; a sheet of paper is not a machine)**

Answers for page 7: 1. B, 2. J, 3. A, 4. J

Review Words   impatient • appliance • appropriate • mumble

Fill in the bubble next to the correct answer.

1. **Which of these words has about the same meaning as *appropriate*?**
   Ⓐ wrong
   Ⓑ right
   Ⓒ quiet
   Ⓓ noisy

2. **When you *mumble*, you don't ___ clearly.**
   Ⓕ hear
   Ⓖ see
   Ⓗ write
   Ⓙ speak

3. **Which of these do *impatient* people dislike?**
   Ⓐ waiting in line
   Ⓑ eating breakfast
   Ⓒ playing in the park
   Ⓓ watching a movie

4. **Which of these is a kitchen *appliance*?**
   Ⓕ a table
   Ⓖ a spoon
   Ⓗ dishwashing soap
   Ⓙ a microwave

Writing

How can you tell when someone is feeling impatient? Use **impatient** in your sentence.

_____

_____

prepare

verb

You **prepare** when you get ready for something.

I studied my math problems to **prepare** for the test.

Which of these show that you have **prepared**?

- You don't know where your homework is.
- You know how to call 911 in an emergency.
- You learn your spelling words before the test.
- You choose your clothes for school the night before.
- You haven't learned your address or phone number yet.

How do you **prepare** for school the night before so that you're ready to go in the morning?

drought

noun

A **drought** is an unusually long period of dry weather.

After months of **drought**, all of the farmer's crops died.

Which of these can be expected during a **drought**?

- floods
- sunshine
- dry weather
- rainstorms
- windblown dust

How would a **drought** affect you if your family was planning a camping or fishing trip at a lake?

A Word a Day • EMC 2793 • © Evan-Moor Corp.

fragile

adjective

Something **fragile** is delicate and easily broken.

The **fragile** vase broke when it fell on the tile floor.

Which words mean about the same as **fragile**?

- weak
- tough
- strong
- breakable
- indestructible

How do you feel when you are around lots of **fragile** objects? How do you act?

spectacular

adjective

Something that is unusually amazing is **spectacular**.

The glowing orange sunset was the most **spectacular** I'd ever seen.

Which of these are **spectacular**?

- a paper clip
- a mud puddle
- a fireworks display
- a double rainbow
- a New Year's Day parade

Tell about the most **spectacular** thing you've ever seen or would like to see.

Review

prepare • drought • fragile • spectacular

Write on the board the four words studied this week. Read the words with the class and briefly review their meanings. Then conduct the oral activities below.

1 Tell students that you are going to give them a clue about one of the words for the week. They are to find the word that answers the clue.

- It rains very little or not at all during one of these. **(a drought)**

- This word describes something that can break very easily. **(fragile)**

- This word describes something that is amazing and wondrous to see. **(spectacular)**

- When people do this, they get ready. **(prepare)**

2 Read each sentence and ask students to supply the correct word to complete the sentence.

- There was a ____ view from the mountaintop. **(spectacular)**

- Be careful! That china cup is ____. **(fragile)**

- We will ____ for the trip by packing our suitcases. **(prepare)**

- After the ____ was over, it was all right to water our lawn again. **(drought)**

3 Read each sentence and ask students to tell which word is wrong. Then have them provide the correct word from the week's list.

- During the flood, our lawn became dry and brown. **(flood/drought)**

- Please don't handle that sturdy glass statue—you might break it. **(sturdy/fragile)**

- The Grand Canyon is a boring sight that amazes everyone. **(boring/spectacular)**

4 Read each sentence and ask students to decide if it is true or false. If the sentence is false, instruct students to explain why.

- Fragile objects don't break. **(false; fragile objects break very easily)**

- A drought can ruin farmers' crops. **(true)**

- You prepare for a trip after you come back home. **(false; you prepare for a trip before you leave)**

- From the tops of most skyscrapers, people can see spectacular views. **(true)**

Answers for page 11: 1. C, 2. J, 3. A, 4. H

| **Review Words** | prepare • drought • fragile • spectacular |

Fill in the bubble next to the correct answer.

1. Which of these words has about the same meaning as *fragile*?

Ⓐ beautiful

Ⓑ broken

Ⓒ delicate

Ⓓ squishy

2. A *spectacular* sight ___ most people.

Ⓕ scares

Ⓖ bores

Ⓗ saddens

Ⓙ amazes

3. To *prepare* for a test, you should ___.

Ⓐ study and get plenty of sleep

Ⓑ get a good grade

Ⓒ keep your eyes on your own paper

Ⓓ play sports or ride your bike

4. Which of these sentences tells about a *drought*?

Ⓕ It rained so hard that the road flooded.

Ⓖ A snowstorm made it dangerous to drive.

Ⓗ After months without rain, many crops died.

Ⓙ We flew our kites on a windy day in March.

Writing

Tell what you would do to prepare to travel a long distance. Use **prepare** in your sentence.

_____

_____

scold

verb

When you **scold** someone, you tell the person in an angry way that he or she did something wrong.

The teacher had to **scold** her students for their rude behavior during the assembly.

Which statements might parents make when they **scold** their children?

- "Your room looks terrific!"
- "You know better than that!"
- "Please don't ever do that again!"
- "You did a great job on that report!"
- "How many times have I asked you not to do that?"

Tell about a time when you were **scolded** for something. What happened?

considerate

adjective

A **considerate** person is kind to others and thoughtful.

The **considerate** boy brought his mother tea when she was sick in bed.

Which of these show **considerate** behavior?

- pushing in line
- sending a get-well card
- yelling at someone who bothers you
- helping to clear the dishes after dinner
- offering to show a new student around school

Tell about a time when someone was **considerate** toward you. How did it make you feel?

instruct

verb

When you **instruct**, you teach something to someone.

My uncle is a lifeguard, so he can **instruct** me on pool safety.

Which of the following mean about the same as **instruct**?

- train
- tutor
- learn
- coach
- study

Think about a special skill or talent you have. How would you **instruct** others so they could also learn that skill?

canine

noun

An animal that belongs to the dog family is a **canine**.

It's not hard to see that dogs and wolves are both **canines**.

Which of the following belong to a **canine**?

- fur
- claws
- scales
- fangs
- feathers

If you owned a **canine**, what would you do to care for it?

scold • considerate • instruct • canine

Write on the board the four words studied this week. Read the words with the class and briefly review their meanings. Then conduct the oral activities below.

1 Tell students that you are going to give them a clue about one of the words for the week. They are to find the word that answers the clue.

- A dog is one, and so is a wolf. **(a canine)**

- If you do nice things for others, this word describes you. **(considerate)**

- Teachers and college professors do this. **(instruct)**

- If a friend broke your favorite toy, you might do this to him or her. **(scold that person)**

2 Read each sentence and ask students to supply the correct word to complete the sentence.

- Thanks for the get-well card! It was very ____ of you to send it. **(considerate)**

- My parents will probably ____ me if I get home late without phoning them. **(scold)**

- A wild ____ lives in a pack of adults and pups. **(canine)**

- Today our teacher will ____ us on some new vocabulary words. **(instruct)**

3 Read each sentence and ask students to tell which word is wrong. Then have them provide the correct word from the week's list.

- The dingo, an Australian wild dog, looks like other felines. **(felines/canines)**

- If you don't do your chores right away, Mom will praise you. **(praise/scold)**

- Thanks! It was so selfish of you to bring me a gift. **(selfish/considerate)**

4 Read each sentence and ask students to decide if it is true or false. If the sentence is false, instruct students to explain why.

- A soccer coach instructs players on ways to score goals. **(true)**

- Wild dogs and pet dogs are both canines. **(true)**

- When a father feels proud of his daughter, he scolds her. **(false; people scold others for behaving badly, not for doing well)**

- It is considerate to ask how someone is feeling. **(true)**

Answers for page 15: 1. B, 2. H, 3. C, 4. J

Review Words   scold • considerate • instruct • canine

Fill in the bubble next to the correct answer.

1. Which of these words has about the same meaning as *instruct*?

Ⓐ learn

Ⓑ teach

Ⓒ join

Ⓓ quit

2. A *considerate* person is ____.

Ⓕ shy around strangers

Ⓖ afraid of animals

Ⓗ careful not to hurt someone's feelings

Ⓙ careful to keep his or her clothes clean

3. Most parents would *scold* their children for ____.

Ⓐ getting good grades in school

Ⓑ making their beds in the morning

Ⓒ fighting with their brothers and sisters

Ⓓ feeding the family dog

4. Which of these sentences tells about a *canine*?

Ⓕ Our living room sofa is old and comfortable.

Ⓖ On Saturday mornings, my dad makes waffles.

Ⓗ My cat likes to sit on top of the refrigerator.

Ⓙ We got a new puppy and named her Holly.

Writing

Tell about a dog that you know. It could be your own dog or a friend's. Use **canine** in your sentence.

_____

_____

increase

verb

You **increase** something when you make or get more of it.

My dad said he'd **increase** my allowance if I started doing more chores.

In which of these situations is something being **increased**?

- The principal makes recess ten minutes longer.
- Mom gives me two scoops of ice cream instead of three.
- I use a pump to add more air to my bike tires.
- We get 100 new books for the school library.
- Dad slows down the car for a stoplight.

What would you like to **increase** at school so that you could have more of it?

annual

adjective

An **annual** event happens every year.

Our family gathers every June for the **annual** Chávez family reunion.

Which of the following are **annual** events?

- Saturday
- a rainy day
- your birthday
- New Year's Day
- the Fourth of July

What's your favorite **annual** event? What do you like about it?

orbit

noun

The path that the Earth or another planet travels around the sun is its **orbit**.

Scientists learn more about a planet by observing its **orbit**.

Which of these have an **orbit**?

- a planet
- the sun
- the moon
- a balloon
- the ocean

What tools might scientists use to follow a planet's **orbit**?

commence

verb

When you **commence**, you begin something.

When the players have finished warming up, the ballgame will **commence**.

Which of these mean about the same as **commence**?

- stop
- start
- halt
- get going
- finish

When do you **commence** getting ready for bed on school nights?

increase • annual • orbit • commence

Write on the board the four words studied this week. Read the words with the class and briefly review their meanings. Then conduct the oral activities below.

1 Tell students that you are going to give them a clue about one of the words for the week. They are to find the word that answers the clue.

- If something happens once a year, it is this kind of event. **(annual)**

- Earth has one of these, and Mars has one, too. **(an orbit)**

- You do this when you begin doing something. **(commence)**

- To go faster, you must do this to your speed. **(increase it)**

2 Read each sentence and ask students to supply the correct word to complete the sentence.

- The Harvest Festival is an _____ event that our town celebrates in October. **(annual)**

- Each planet's _____ takes it around the sun. **(orbit)**

- Thousands of fans waited for the baseball game to _____. **(commence)**

- Don't _____ the amount of sugar in the recipe, or the pie will be too sweet. **(increase)**

3 Read each sentence and ask students to tell which word is wrong. Then have them provide the correct word from the week's list.

- It's the moment we've all been waiting for: The show is about to end! **(end/commence)**

- I hope you will come to our weekly holiday banquet in December. **(weekly/annual)**

- Great news! The boss has decided to lower Mom's salary! **(lower/increase)**

4 Read each sentence and ask students to decide if it is true or false. If the sentence is false, instruct students to explain why.

- Saturn's orbit takes it around the Earth. **(false; its orbit takes it around the sun)**

- If we increase the number of kids in our school, we'll have more kids than before. **(true)**

- Thanksgiving is an annual event. **(true)**

- When a journey commences, it ends. **(false; it begins)**

Answers for page 19: 1. D, 2. J, 3. B, 4. G

Review Words   increase • annual • orbit • commence

Fill in the bubble next to the correct answer.

1. Which word means the opposite of *commence*?

Ⓐ purchase

Ⓑ sell

Ⓒ begin

Ⓓ halt

2. An *annual* event happens ____ .

Ⓕ every day

Ⓖ once a week

Ⓗ once a month

Ⓙ once a year

3. Mercury's *orbit* is the path in which it travels around ____ .

Ⓐ the moon

Ⓑ the sun

Ⓒ the North Pole

Ⓓ the Earth

4. What happens when a cat's weight *increases*?

Ⓕ The cat gets thinner.

Ⓖ The cat gains weight.

Ⓗ The cat's weight stays the same.

Ⓙ The cat's fur grows longer.

Writing

What is something that you would like to be an annual event in your life? Why?
Use **annual** in your sentence.

_____

_____

locate

verb

When you find something, you **locate** it.

I couldn't **locate** my favorite shirt, but then I found it in a basket of clean laundry.

Where would you **locate**:

- your bike?
- your shoes?
- your backpack?
- your favorite toy?
- your homework?

What do you do when you can't **locate** something that you need?

possession

noun

Something that belongs to you is your **possession**.

I keep my **possessions** on my side of the room, and my sister keeps hers on her side.

To whom do each of these **possessions** belong?

- the car
- your house
- your backpack
- your brush and comb
- your best friend's bike

Tell about one of your favorite **possessions**.
Where did you get it, and how do you care for it?

significant

adjective

If something is **significant**, it has importance.

My mom writes about all the **significant** events in my life in my baby book: my first steps, my first loose tooth, my first day of school, and others.

Which of these are **significant**?

- turning 90 years old
- changing a light bulb
- graduating from high school
- riding a bike alone for the first time
- eating a peanut butter and jelly sandwich

Tell about a **significant** event in your life and how it changed you or those people around you.

ascend

verb

When you **ascend**, you go up.

The airplane took off and **ascended** through the clouds.

Which of these could you **ascend**?

- a rug
- a ladder
- the stairs
- a mountain
- a birthday cake

Imagine that you have just **ascended** in a hot-air balloon. Describe what you think the view is from the sky.

locate • possession • significant • ascend

Write on the board the four words studied this week. Read the words with the class and briefly review their meanings. Then conduct the oral activities below.

1 Tell students that you are going to give them a clue about one of the words for the week. They are to find the word that answers the clue.

- This is something that someone owns. **(a possession)**

- When people go up in hot-air balloons, they do this. **(ascend)**

- You could use this word to describe an important idea or happening. **(significant)**

- You do this when you find your lost sweater. **(locate it)**

2 Read each sentence and ask students to supply the correct word to complete the sentence.

- When I was three years old, my blue blanket was my most prized ____. **(possession)**

- After planes take off, they ____ until they are thousands of feet in the air. **(ascend)**

- Please ____ your library books so we can return them. **(locate)**

- The Fourth of July is a very ____ date in United States history. **(significant)**

3 Read each sentence and ask students to tell which word or words are wrong. Then have them provide the correct word from the week's list.

- Please lose your backpack so we can leave for school. **(lose/locate)**

- My cousin's wedding was an unimportant event for our family. **(an unimportant/a significant)**

- If you want to go down from the first floor to the fifth, you can use the elevator or the stairs. **(go down/ascend)**

4 Read each sentence and ask students to decide if it is true or false. If the sentence is false, instruct students to explain why.

- Your possessions are things that belong to someone else. **(false; they belong to you)**

- To locate something, you need to look for it. **(true)**

- After a balloon pops, it ascends. **(false; it doesn't go up, it falls)**

- Your birthday is a significant date for you. **(true)**

Answers for page 23: 1. C, 2. F, 3. B, 4. G

| **Review Words** | locate • possession • significant • ascend |

Fill in the bubble next to the correct answer.

1. Which word means the opposite of *ascend*?
Ⓐ shrink
Ⓑ float
Ⓒ sink
Ⓓ rise

2. Every *significant* event is ___.
Ⓓ important
Ⓖ unimportant
Ⓗ joyful
Ⓘ sorrowful

3. When you *locate* a library book, you ___ it.
Ⓐ read
Ⓑ find
Ⓒ return
Ⓓ damage

4. Which of these is Mr. Ginsburg's *possession*?
Ⓓ his mother or father
Ⓖ his winter coat
Ⓗ his mood today
Ⓘ his son or daughter

| **Writing** |

Tell about a possession you had before you were five years old. Use **possession** in your sentence.

_____

_____

browse

verb

You **browse** when you look at something in a casual way.

My mom didn't want to buy any books at the bookstore; she just wanted to **browse**.

Which of these mean about the same as **browse**?

- look around
- surf the Internet
- study
- glance through
- examine

Tell about something you like to **browse** through.

cautious

adjective

When you're very careful and don't take any chances, you're being **cautious**.

We had to be **cautious** on the drive to school because there were many potholes.

In which of these situations should you be **cautious**?

- when you eat a cookie
- when you pour hot liquid
- when you use a sharp knife
- when you quietly read a book
- when you cross a busy street

Tell about a time when you had to be **cautious** about something. What did you do, and how did it turn out?

elderly

adjective

A person is **elderly** if he or she is quite old.

The **elderly** woman was 85 when she took her first airplane trip!

Which of these could describe an **elderly** person?

- wise
- babyish
- athletic
- experienced
- white-haired

Tell about something you've learned from an **elderly** person.

eliminate

verb

If you get rid of something, you **eliminate** it.

After we rake the leaves, we can **eliminate** that chore from our list.

Which of these would you like to **eliminate**?

- recess
- homework
- washing dishes
- after-school snacks
- making your bed every day

If you could **eliminate** one thing from your day, what would it be and why?

browse • cautious • elderly • eliminate

Write on the board the four words studied this week. Read the words with the class and briefly review their meanings. Then conduct the oral activities below.

1 Tell students that you are going to give them a clue about one of the words for the week. They are to find the word that answers the clue.

- If there was a bad smell in your home, you would probably want to do this to it. **(eliminate it)**

- This word might describe a great-grandparent. **(elderly)**

- You might do this at a bookstore or a library. **(browse)**

- This word describes the way you would act to avoid danger. **(cautious)**

2 Read each sentence and ask students to supply the correct word to complete the sentence.

- Grandma Liz is an ____ woman of 75. **(elderly)**

- Please be very ____ when you open a hot oven. **(cautious)**

- Sometimes I ____ through magazines without reading them. **(browse)**

- "Buy Minty Fresh Mouthwash and ____ bad breath!" **(eliminate)**

3 Read each sentence and ask students to tell which word or words are wrong. Then have them provide the correct word from the week's list.

- Be careless when you use sharp knives. **(careless/cautious)**

- "To create unpleasant odors, use Pine Forest Air Freshener!" **(create/eliminate)**

- My great-grandfather is very young and will soon turn 90. **(very young/elderly)**

4 Read each sentence and ask students to decide if it is true or false. If the sentence is false, instruct students to explain why.

- When you browse through a store, you know exactly what you came to buy. **(false; when you browse through a store, you look casually around)**

- Cautious people are less likely to get hurt than careless ones. **(true)**

- Some elderly people need canes to help them walk. **(true)**

- Opening windows can help to eliminate bad smells. **(true)**

Answers for page 27: 1. A, 2. H, 3. D, 4. H

Name _____

Fill in the bubble next to the correct answer.

1. Which word means the opposite of *cautious*?
- Ⓐ careless
- Ⓑ restless
- Ⓒ thoughtless
- Ⓓ sleepless

2. Which word means the opposite of *elderly*?
- Ⓕ ancient
- Ⓖ enormous
- Ⓗ young
- Ⓙ sorrowful

3. When you *eliminate* a problem, you ____ .
- Ⓐ don't admit that anything is wrong
- Ⓑ ask someone for help
- Ⓒ make it worse
- Ⓓ get rid of it

4. Which of these might someone *browse* through?
- Ⓕ some friends
- Ⓖ a pair of shoes
- Ⓗ a clothing store
- Ⓙ the kitchen sink

Writing

Describe a friend or a family member who is elderly. Use **elderly** in your sentence.

_____

_____

stoop

verb

You **stoop** when you squat down or bend over.

Natalie had to **stoop** to pick up the pencil that she dropped on the floor.

Would you have to **stoop** to:

- reach the highest book on the shelf?
- pick up the cat dish to fill it with water?
- pick up the newspaper in the driveway?
- tie your shoelace?
- catch a balloon that floated up and away?

What is something in your classroom that you have to **stoop** to reach?

transparent

adjective

Something is **transparent** if light goes through it and you can see through it.

We watched the fish at the aquarium through a large **transparent** window.

Which of the following are **transparent**?

- a brick
- a book
- a fishbowl
- a car windshield
- a pair of glasses

What do you have that's **transparent**? What is it made of?

accurate

adjective

Something is **accurate** if it has no mistakes.

John was **accurate** in his spelling of all the words and got an A on his test.

In which of these situations is it important to be **accurate**?

- giving change to a customer
- putting a jigsaw puzzle together
- taking medicine that the doctor prescribed
- throwing clothing in the laundry basket
- giving your address to the 911 operator during a home emergency

When is it important to be **accurate** in school? What would happen if you were not accurate in those situations?

fiction

noun

Fiction is writing that tells about characters and events that are not real.

I wrote a story about a princess and a magic chicken for the **fiction** contest.

Which of the following are examples of **fiction**?

- *The Three Little Pigs*
- a book about a talking duck
- the life story of Abraham Lincoln
- a book of facts about snakes and lizards
- the story of how electricity was discovered

What's your favorite **fiction** story? Why do you like it? Do you prefer **fiction** or nonfiction when you choose something to read? Why?

Review

stoop • transparent • accurate • fiction

Write on the board the four words studied this week. Read the words with the class and briefly review their meanings. Then conduct the oral activities below.

1 Tell students that you are going to give them a clue about one of the words for the week. They are to find the word that answers the clue.

- Glass and clear plastic are this way. (**transparent**)

- If you dropped a coin, you might do this so that you could pick it up. (**stoop**)

- This word would describe a correct answer to a math problem. (**accurate**)

- This is a name for made-up stories. (**fiction**)

2 Read each sentence and ask students to supply the correct word to complete the sentence.

- You added the numbers correctly, so your answer is ____. (**accurate**)

- Fairy tales and tall tales are ____. (**fiction**)

- The vase was ____, so we could see the colored marbles at the bottom. (**transparent**)

- Mr. Wu had to ____ to pick up his two-year-old son. (**stoop**)

3 Read each sentence and ask students to tell which word or words are wrong. Then have them provide the correct word from the week's list.

- I stand on tiptoe to pull weeds out of the soil in my garden. (**stand on tiptoe/stoop**)

- Yes, that is incorrect: 8 plus 8 does equal 16. (**incorrect/accurate**)

- Beverly Cleary wrote true stories about two imaginary sisters. (**true/fiction**)

4 Read each sentence and ask students to decide if it is true or false. If the sentence is false, instruct students to explain why.

- You can't see through transparent plastic. (**false; you can see through transparent materials**)

- It is accurate to say that the sun is many times as large as Earth. (**true**)

- An author must use imagination to write fiction. (**true**)

- When you stoop, you stand up straight and tall. (**false; when you stoop, you squat down low**)

Answers for page 31: 1. D, 2. H, 3. C, 4. J

Review Words	stoop • transparent • accurate • fiction

Fill in the bubble next to the correct answer.

1. Which word means the opposite of *accurate*?

Ⓐ messy

Ⓑ enormous

Ⓒ unhelpful

Ⓓ incorrect

2. Which word has about the same meaning as *stoop*?

Ⓕ stretch

Ⓖ sprint

Ⓗ squat

Ⓙ twist

3. Which is *transparent*?

Ⓐ a wooden bowl

Ⓑ a metal spoon

Ⓒ plastic wrap

Ⓓ a china plate

4. Which of these is a work of *fiction*?

Ⓕ an article on endangered frogs

Ⓖ a science book about frogs

Ⓗ a photo of a rainforest frog

Ⓙ a story about a talking frog

Writing

What is the last fiction book you read? Would you recommend it to a friend?
Use **fiction** in your sentence.

_____

_____

irritable

adjective

An **irritable** person is grumpy and gets mad easily.

I get **irritable** when I'm tired and hungry. It's best to leave me alone when I'm like that!

Would you be **irritable** if:

- mosquitoes were biting you?
- your favorite movie was on TV?
- you were going out for ice cream?
- your baby sister spilled milk all over you?
- you were trying to read and someone kept interrupting you?

What makes you **irritable**? What do you do when you start feeling that way? What makes you feel better?

mob

noun

A **mob** is a large, often disorderly crowd.

Police officers tried to control the **mob** that was waiting for the rock star to arrive.

Which of these describe a **mob**?

- your family at the dinner table
- a child feeding a duck at the park
- a crowd of shoppers waiting for the doors at the mall to open
- two children sharing a sandwich on the bench at school recess
- a large group of people waiting to buy tickets at the opening of baseball season

Tell about a time when you've seen a **mob**. What were the people doing? How might it be dangerous to be in or near a **mob**?

launch

verb

When you set a vehicle in motion into the water or air, you **launch** it.

The space shuttle will **launch** into space next week if the weather is clear.

Which of these could you **launch**?

- a cup
- a car
- a ship
- a rocket
- a telephone

Have you ever built something and **launched** it? If so, tell about it. If not, what would you like to make and **launch**?

fidgety

adjective

Someone who is **fidgety** has trouble staying still.

The toddlers could sit still for only a few minutes before they got **fidgety**.

Which of these mean about the same as **fidgety**?

- restless
- squirmy
- bored
- calm
- still

When have you felt yourself getting **fidgety**? What can you do to stop yourself from being **fidgety**?

irritable • mob • launch • fidgety

Write on the board the four words studied this week. Read the words with the class and briefly review their meanings. Then conduct the oral activities below.

1 Tell students that you are going to give them a clue about one of the words for the week. They are to find the word that answers the clue.

- This word describes you if you can't sit still. (**fidgety**)

- You're this way if you feel grumpy and grouchy. (**irritable**)

- This is a large, noisy crowd of people. (**a mob**)

- You could do this to a paper airplane. (**launch it**)

2 Read each sentence and ask students to supply the correct word to complete the sentence.

- Please stop being so ____, and sit still! (**fidgety**)

- When I'm ____, I hate listening to my baby sister's squeaky toys. (**irritable**)

- A ____ crowded around the movie star's car. (**mob**)

- Workers will ____ a satellite into space at noon. (**launch**)

3 Read each sentence and ask students to tell which word is wrong. Then have them provide the correct word from the week's list.

- I can tell that you are nervous about your performance, because you are so calm. (**calm/fidgety**)

- When I feel cheerful, my brother's loud chewing makes me want to scream. (**cheerful/irritable**)

- A pair of fans wanting autographs crowded around the winning soccer team as it left the field. (**pair/mob**)

- To test the rocket engine, NASA will store it. (**store/launch**)

4 Read each sentence and ask students to decide if it is true or false. If the sentence is false, instruct students to explain why.

- People can launch boats and rockets. (**true**)

- There are about three or four people in a mob. (**false; a mob is a large crowd**)

- When someone is irritable, almost anything can make that person mad. (**true**)

- A fidgety boy might squirm around, tap his feet, or make noises with his mouth. (**true**)

Answers for page 35: 1. A, 2. J, 3. D, 4. G

Review Words	irritable • mob • launch • fidgety

Fill in the bubble next to the correct answer.

1. Which word means the opposite of *irritable*?
Ⓐ cheerful
Ⓑ healthy
Ⓒ moist
Ⓓ smooth

2. Which word has about the same meaning as *mob*?
Ⓕ pair
Ⓖ trio
Ⓗ audience
Ⓙ crowd

3. When workers *launch* a space shuttle, they _____ .
Ⓐ bring it back to Earth
Ⓑ take it apart for repairs
Ⓒ paint it red, white, and blue
Ⓓ fire it into space

4. Which sentence tells about a *fidgety* person?
Ⓕ Katrina sat calmly and quietly in her chair.
Ⓖ Matty kept squirming and tapping her foot.
Ⓗ Jack fell fast asleep on the living room couch.
Ⓙ Bo played soccer with a bunch of other kids.

Writing

Would you like to be inside a space shuttle as it blasts off? Why or why not? Use **launch** in your sentence.

_____

_____

independent

adjective

When you think and act for yourself, you're being **independent**.

My 90-year-old great-grandma is still **independent**. She lives alone and cooks and cleans for herself.

Would you be **independent** if you:

- had your best friend choose the color of your new bike?
- finished your homework by yourself?
- needed help to make your bed?
- made your own breakfast?
- chose your own clothes?

In what ways are you **independent**? In what ways are you not **independent** yet?

inflate

verb

If you fill something with air or gas, you **inflate** it.

The coach forgot to **inflate** the ball, so it was too flat to bounce.

Which of these could you **inflate**?

- a table
- a football
- a baseball
- a telephone
- a hot-air balloon

Have you ever **inflated** a ball, balloon, or bike tire? Did you use a pump or your lungs? Tell about how the thing you were **inflating** changed.

adjustable

adjective

Something is **adjustable** if it can be changed to make it fit or work better.

An **adjustable** chair can go up or down to fit people of different heights.

Which of these are **adjustable**?

- a belt
- a sock
- a radio
- an earring
- an antenna

What article of clothing do you have that's **adjustable**? What furniture or appliances do you have that are **adjustable**? In what ways are they **adjustable**?

astonish

verb

If you greatly surprise someone, you **astonish** them.

We were **astonished** when the magician pulled ten rabbits out of his hat.

Would it **astonish** you to see someone:

- yawn?
- get shot out of a cannon?
- brush their teeth?
- walk on their hands?
- twist their body into a pretzel shape?

Tell about a time when something **astonished** you. What was it and how did you feel?

independent • inflate • adjustable • astonish

Write on the board the four words studied this week. Read the words with the class and briefly review their meanings. Then conduct the oral activities below.

1 Tell students that you are going to give them a clue about one of the words for the week. They are to find the word that answers the clue.

- This word describes people who make their own decisions. (**independent**)

- You might do this to a beach ball if it was flat. (**inflate it**)

- This word describes something that you can move into different positions. (**adjustable**)

- If you leaped over a six-foot-high fence, you might do this to people. (**astonish them**)

2 Read each sentence and ask students to supply the correct word to complete the sentence.

- It will ____ you to learn that some people have never seen computers. (**astonish**)

- Please ____ my bike tires. They are completely flat. (**inflate**)

- My sister wishes she were more ____ so she wouldn't have to follow Mom's rules. (**independent**)

- This table is ____. You can raise or lower it. (**adjustable**)

3 Read each list of words and phrases. Ask students to supply the word that fits best with each.

- tire, beach ball, air mattress, blow up, fill with gas (**inflate**)

- on your own, making your own decisions, free (**independent**)

- greatly surprise, amaze, flabbergast (**astonish**)

- raise and lower, furniture, seat belt (**adjustable**)

4 Read each sentence and ask students to decide if it is true or false. If the sentence is false, instruct students to explain why.

- Most children get more independent as they grow older. (**true**)

- Seat belts are adjustable. (**true**)

- Usual events astonish people. (**false; greatly surprising events astonish people**)

- Some people inflate their car tires at gas stations. (**true**)

Answers for page 39: 1. A, 2. F, 3. B, 4. G

| **Review Words** | independent • inflate • adjustable • astonish |

Fill in the bubble next to the correct answer.

1. **Which sentence tells about an *independent* decision?**
   Ⓐ Shelby will decide whether to join the team.
   Ⓑ Taylor's mom will choose her school clothes.
   Ⓒ Pablo's dad decided that his son would play baseball.
   Ⓓ Ana's mom decided that Ana could watch TV.

2. **Which word has about the same meaning as *astonish*?**
   Ⓕ surprise
   Ⓖ trick
   Ⓗ frighten
   Ⓙ instruct

3. **When you *inflate* your bike's tires, you _____ .**
   Ⓐ buy new ones
   Ⓑ fill them with air
   Ⓒ let the air out of them
   Ⓓ fill them with water

4. **Which sentence tells about an *adjustable* piece of furniture?**
   Ⓕ Our living room sofa is old and comfortable.
   Ⓖ Mom can raise or lower her office chair.
   Ⓗ This armchair is covered in red plaid cloth.
   Ⓙ This wooden chair is almost 100 years old.

Writing

When you become completely independent, what do you want to do?
Use **independent** in your sentence.

_____

_____

statement

noun

You make a **statement** when you tell about or explain something.

Everyone waited for the president to make a **statement** about the peace agreement.

Which of the following are **statements**?

- "Can we go?"
- "I don't like spinach."
- "My favorite color is red."
- "I have a new baby sister."
- "Would you like some ice cream?"

Make a **statement** about what you like best in school. Then ask someone else to make a **statement**.

charity

noun

A **charity** is a group that collects money or things to help needy people.

The children gave some toys to a **charity** that sends them to sick children.

Which of the following might a **charity** do?

- pay for poor children's operations
- give money to rich, famous people
- give homeless families a warm place to sleep
- cook meals for people who have nothing to eat
- hold a contest to see who is the most talented singer

If you could organize people to give things to a **charity**, what would you want to collect, and which **charity** would you give those things to?

disposable

adjective

Something is **disposable** if you can throw it away after using it.

It's better for the environment to clean up spills with cloth towels instead of **disposable** paper towels.

Which of the following are **disposable**?

- bed sheets
- computers
- paper napkins
- cloth diapers
- paper drinking cups

What do you have in your lunch that's **disposable**? What do you have that can be reused? Do you think it's better for our planet to use **disposable** or reusable things?

ancient

adjective

If something is **ancient**, it is extremely old.

The king wore an **ancient** crown that had been handed down in his family for generations.

Which of these might be displayed in a museum of **ancient** history?

- a fossil
- a computer game
- a solar-powered car
- an Egyptian mummy
- stones from a temple built 6,000 years ago

What is something **ancient** that you have seen? Where did you see it?

statement • charity • disposable • ancient

Write on the board the four words studied this week. Read the words with the class and briefly review their meanings. Then conduct the oral activities below.

1 Tell students that you are going to give them a clue about one of the words for the week. They are to find the word that answers the clue.

- You might donate used clothes and toys to one. **(a charity)**

- You could use this word to describe paper towels and paper napkins. **(disposable)**

- You could use this word to describe fossils. **(ancient)**

- This is not a question, but it is something you might say or write. **(a statement)**

2 Read each sentence and ask students to supply the correct word to complete the sentence.

- The presidential candidate made a ___ about health care. **(statement)**

- The bristlecone pine tree is an ___ species that can live for thousands of years. **(ancient)**

- We took some ___ paper napkins on our picnic. **(disposable)**

- This ___ saves animals during disasters such as wildfires and floods. **(charity)**

3 Read each list of words and phrases. Ask students to supply the word that fits best with each.

- throw away, paper towels, paper cups, tissues **(disposable)**

- dinosaur fossils, redwood forests, extremely old **(ancient)**

- helps needy people, collects donations, Red Cross **(charity)**

- express ideas and feelings, say something, declaration **(statement)**

4 Read each sentence and ask students to decide if it is true or false. If the sentence is false, instruct students to explain why.

- Charities are businesses like grocery stores. **(false; charities use the money they raise to help people)**

- The principal of a school might make a statement about playground rules. **(true)**

- Most disposable items are only used once. **(true)**

- Human beings lived on Earth during ancient times. **(true)**

Answers for page 43: 1. C, 2. H, 3. B, 4. H

Review Words   statement • charity • disposable • ancient

Fill in the bubble next to the correct answer.

1. Which sentence is a *statement* you might hear at the library?

Ⓐ "Where are the books on the solar system?"

Ⓑ "You may talk as loudly as you wish."

Ⓒ "You may check out four books at a time."

Ⓓ "Do you have a current library card?"

2. Which word means the opposite of *ancient*?

Ⓕ tall

Ⓖ short

Ⓗ modern

Ⓙ old

3. A *charity* is a group that ____.

Ⓐ sells groceries

Ⓑ helps those in need

Ⓒ entertains people

Ⓓ gets together for fun

4. Which sentence tells about something *disposable*?

Ⓕ Please put the cups and plates in the dishwasher.

Ⓖ Let's buy a comfortable new couch for the living room.

Ⓗ Please use this paper towel to wipe off the counter.

Ⓙ Our outdoor chairs are made of white plastic.

Writing

What ancient objects might you find in a museum? Use **ancient** in your sentence.

_____

_____

fragrance

noun

A **fragrance** is a sweet, pleasant smell.

As we walked through the rose garden, we enjoyed the **fragrance** of the many open blossoms.

Which of these have a **fragrance**?

- water
- a rose
- a skunk
- perfume
- freshly baked cookies

What **fragrances** do you enjoy? Do you prefer the **fragrance** of perfume or the natural **fragrance** of flowers?

vanish

verb

If you disappear suddenly, you **vanish**.

The moon **vanished** behind the clouds.

Which of these mean about the same as **vanish**?

- go
- leave
- appear
- show up
- fade away

If you had the power to make one thing **vanish** so that the world would become a better place, what would you choose?

reasonable

adjective

Something that is fair and makes sense is **reasonable**.

The produce prices at the farmers' market are more **reasonable** than supermarket prices.

Would it be **reasonable** to:

- eat only dessert?
- keep an elephant as a pet?
- sleep only two hours each night?
- wear a warm jacket in the winter?
- eat a good breakfast before school?

Tell about a time when someone asked you to do something that was **reasonable**. Then think of a time when someone expected something that was not **reasonable**. What did you do?

anticipate

verb

If you **anticipate** something, you expect it to happen and are prepared for it.

The weather forecast said to **anticipate** a storm, so we got our rain gear ready.

Which events might you want to **anticipate** and be prepared for?

- a power outage
- the daily mail delivery
- a difficult spelling test
- your cousins' annual visit
- a flood of the nearby river

What is something you **anticipate** each year, and how do you get ready for it?

Review

fragrance • vanish • reasonable • anticipate

Write on the board the four words studied this week. Read the words with the class and briefly review their meanings. Then conduct the oral activities below.

1 Tell students that you are going to give them a clue about one of the words for the week. They are to find the word that answers the clue.

- When things disappear, they do this. (**vanish**)

- Roses and freshly baked bread each have this. (**a fragrance**)

- You do this if you expect an event to happen. (**anticipate it**)

- When you act sensibly, this word accurately describes you. (**reasonable**)

2 Read each sentence and ask students to supply the correct word to complete the sentence.

- Please be ____! You aren't making sense right now. (**reasonable**)

- My parents ____ that I will go to college someday. (**anticipate**)

- Mmm! What is that wonderful ____ that I smell? (**fragrance**)

- The rabbit ran off so quickly that it seemed to ____. (**vanish**)

3 Read each sentence and ask students to tell which word or words are wrong. Then have them provide the correct word from the week's list.

- Nine o'clock is a ridiculous bedtime on school nights. (**ridiculous/reasonable**)

- I love the horrible smell of cookies baking. (**horrible smell/fragrance**)

- "Brite and Kleen Cleaner makes dirt appear!" (**appear/vanish**)

- In May, we excitedly remember summer vacation. (**remember/anticipate**)

4 Read each sentence and ask students to decide if it is true or false. If the sentence is false, instruct students to explain why.

- A reasonable statement is fair and makes sense. (**true**)

- When you anticipate having guests, you expect guests to visit you. (**true**)

- A fragrance is a bad smell. (**false; it is a pleasant smell**)

- To vanish means to slowly walk away. (**false; someone who vanishes disappears quickly**)

Answers for page 47: **1. D, 2. F, 3. C, 4. G**

| **Review Words** | fragrance • vanish • reasonable • anticipate |

Fill in the bubble next to the correct answer.

1. Which word means the opposite of *vanish*?

Ⓐ laugh

Ⓑ help

Ⓒ ruin

Ⓓ appear

2. Which word has about the same meaning as *reasonable*?

Ⓕ sensible

Ⓖ ridiculous

Ⓗ astonishing

Ⓙ confusing

3. When you *anticipate* a rainstorm, you ____ .

Ⓐ hope that it won't rain

Ⓑ explain how hard it rained

Ⓒ expect that it will rain soon

Ⓓ don't believe that it will rain

4. Which sentence tells about a *fragrance*?

Ⓕ Please take out the garbage—it stinks!

Ⓖ Mom's perfume smells just like roses.

Ⓗ Ugh, my cat's breath smells fishy!

Ⓙ When I have a cold, I can't smell anything.

Writing

Tell what the inside of a bakery smells like. Use **fragrance** in your sentence.

_____

_____

withdraw

verb

When you **withdraw** something, you take it away or remove it.

I'm not allowed to **withdraw** money from my savings account at the bank. I can only add money to it.

Which words mean about the same as **withdraw**?

- draw
- enter
- pull out
- take out
- take over

Have you ever joined an activity or a game but then had to **withdraw**? Tell about what happened and why you decided to **withdraw**.

unfortunate

adjective

Something that is **unfortunate** is unlucky.

It was **unfortunate** that Abby forgot to bring her swimsuit to the pool.

Which of the following situations are **unfortunate**?

- getting a new puppy
- winning the schoolwide spelling bee
- your house catching fire and burning
- arriving too late to get a good seat at the movies
- forgetting to turn in the homework that you worked so hard to complete

Tell about a time when something **unfortunate** happened to you or to someone you know. How did you feel?

banquet

noun

A **banquet** is a big, formal meal for many people on a special occasion.

The chef prepared lots of food and a beautiful cake for the wedding **banquet**.

Which of the following might you see at a **banquet**?

- beautiful china dishes
- fine silverware
- crystal goblets
- fast food
- paper cups

Have you ever been to a **banquet**? How is a **banquet** different from dinner at your house?

babble

verb

When you **babble**, you make sounds that don't have any meaning.

When the baby started to **babble**, we knew it wouldn't be long before she'd say her first real words.

Which ones might **babble**?

- a television newscaster
- a teacher giving a spelling test
- a chimp that is mimicking a person
- a person pretending to speak another language
- someone who is so scared that he can barely speak

Tell about a time when you were so scared, nervous, or excited that you started to **babble**.
Why is it hard to understand someone who **babbles**?

withdraw • unfortunate • banquet • babble

Write on the board the four words studied this week. Read the words with the class and briefly review their meanings. Then conduct the oral activities below.

1 Tell students that you are going to give them a clue about one of the words for the week. They are to find the word that answers the clue.

- One-year-old humans and monkeys do this. **(babble)**

- Many weddings include one of these. **(a banquet)**

- When a man takes money out of his bank account, he does this. **(withdraws it)**

- You could use this word to describe someone with bad luck. **(unfortunate)**

2 Read each sentence and ask students to supply the correct word to complete the sentence.

- Mom decided to ____ my sister from her preschool. **(withdraw)**

- When the one-year-old twins ____ at each other, it almost sounds like real words. **(babble)**

- It is ____ that Pablo caught a bad cold right before our trip. **(unfortunate)**

- The parents' club held a ____ at a fancy restaurant to honor the graduating students. **(banquet)**

3 Read each sentence and ask students to tell which word or words are wrong. Then have them provide the correct word from the week's list.

- How lucky you were to break your arm! **(lucky/unfortunate)**

- Mom needs $100 to buy work clothes. She will deposit that much from her bank account. **(deposit/withdraw)**

- I was so nervous about speaking in front of the class that I began to talk perfectly. **(talk perfectly/babble)**

4 Read each sentence and ask students to decide if it is true or false. If the sentence is false, instruct students to explain why.

- A banquet is the same as a snack. **(false; a banquet is a big meal put on for a special occasion)**

- Most babies babble before they begin to say words. **(true)**

- An accident is an unfortunate event. **(true)**

- If you decide not to enter the talent contest, you withdraw your name. **(true)**

Answers for page 51: 1. A, 2. J, 3. B, 4. G

Review Words | withdraw • unfortunate • banquet • babble

Fill in the bubble next to the correct answer.

1. Which word means the opposite of *unfortunate*?
Ⓐ lucky
Ⓑ joyful
Ⓒ healthy
Ⓓ athletic

2. Which word has about the same meaning as *withdraw*?
Ⓕ repair
Ⓖ deposit
Ⓗ ruin
Ⓙ remove

3. When a young child *babbles*, she ____.
Ⓐ speaks very clearly
Ⓑ makes sounds that are not real words
Ⓒ sings songs that she learned in school
Ⓓ scribbles on paper

4. Which sentence tells about a *banquet*?
Ⓕ After school, I love to snack on cheese, crackers, and fruit.
Ⓖ Our soccer team held a fancy dinner to honor our coach.
Ⓗ On weekends, we have pancakes or waffles for breakfast.
Ⓙ My favorite meal includes spaghetti and garlic bread.

Writing

What would you like to eat and drink at a banquet? Use **banquet** in your sentence.

_____

_____

hubbub

noun

A **hubbub** is loud, confused noise.

The blue jays made such a **hubbub** outside my window that they woke me up.

Which of these would make a **hubbub**?

- a purring cat
- a pack of barking dogs
- fans at a basketball game
- a snake gliding through tall grass
- three-year-olds at a birthday party

Tell about a time when you heard a **hubbub**. What was going on? What did you do?

ancestor

noun

An **ancestor** is a family member who lived long ago, even before your grandparents.

My mother's **ancestors** came from Spain, and my father's came from Russia.

Which of the following could be **ancestors**?

- your sister
- your cousin
- your best friend
- your great-grandfather
- your great-great-great aunt

Tell something you know about your **ancestors**, or share something you'd like to learn about them.

quarrel

verb

If you **quarrel** with someone, you argue with words.

My brother and I usually get along, but sometimes we **quarrel** over our chores.

Which of these mean about the same as **quarrel**?

- fight
- share
- agree
- argue
- disagree

Tell about a time when you **quarreled** with someone. How did it end?

prompt

adjective

Someone who is **prompt** is always on time.

A **prompt** student is always in class when the bell rings.

Would it be important to be **prompt** if you:

- had a doctor's appointment?
- had to catch a plane for a trip?
- wanted to see the beginning of a movie?
- could water the plants anytime during the day?
- were going to a school carnival that is going on all day long?

Are you **prompt** getting to school every day? Why is that important? What happens if you are not **prompt** getting to school?

hubbub • ancestor • quarrel • prompt

Write on the board the four words studied this week. Read the words with the class and briefly review their meanings. Then conduct the oral activities below.

1 Tell students that you are going to give them a clue about one of the words for the week. They are to find the word that answers the clue.

- Your great-great-grandpa was one of yours. **(an ancestor)**

- If you get to an appointment on time, this word accurately describes you. **(prompt)**

- Most brothers and sisters do this sometimes. **(quarrel)**

- Five barking dogs in one room would create one of these. **(a hubbub)**

2 Read each sentence and ask students to supply the correct word to complete the sentence.

- Sasha's _____ was an artist who lived in the 1600s. **(ancestor)**

- Thanks for being so _____. Now we can start the meeting on time. **(prompt)**

- Please don't _____! Stop arguing and try to get along. **(quarrel)**

- The ten toddlers at Ana's party created quite a _____. **(hubbub)**

3 Read each sentence and ask students to tell which word or words are wrong. Then have them provide the correct word from the week's list.

- The teacher gave Taylor a gold star for being tardy. **(tardy/prompt)**

- Five sisters share the bathroom, so they often agree on whose turn it is to go next. **(agree on/quarrel about)**

- My nephew was born in 1775. **(nephew/ancestor)**

- The quiet in the bus station made it impossible to have a conversation. **(quiet/hubbub)**

4 Read each sentence and ask students to decide if it is true or false. If the sentence is false, instruct students to explain why.

- Quarreling is the same as arguing. **(true)**

- Most teachers like it when students are prompt. **(true)**

- Your ancestors lived long before you were born. **(true)**

- When a playground is crowded, a hubbub is usually the result. **(true)**

Answers for page 55: 1. A, 2. F, 3. D, 4. H

Name _____

Review Words   hubbub • ancestor • quarrel • prompt

Fill in the bubble next to the correct answer.

1. Which word means the opposite of *prompt*?

Ⓐ tardy

Ⓑ unhealthy

Ⓒ selfish

Ⓓ sorrowful

2. Which word has about the same meaning as *quarrel*?

Ⓕ argue

Ⓖ dance

Ⓗ play

Ⓙ chat

3. Your *ancestor* is a family member who ____.

Ⓐ is your brother's or sister's child

Ⓑ is your mother's or father's parent

Ⓒ lives in your home community

Ⓓ lived before your grandparents

4. Which sentence tells about a *hubbub*?

Ⓕ Everyone was in bed; even the dog was asleep.

Ⓖ Today in class, we silently read our library books.

Ⓗ Last weekend, eight of my cousins came over to play.

Ⓙ My mom and dad had dinner at a quiet restaurant.

Writing

Would you rather play quietly with one friend or be part of a hubbub? Explain why. Use **hubbub** in your sentence.

_____

_____

motion

noun

Motion is any kind of movement.

The rocking **motion** of the ship made it hard to walk without falling.

Which of these are in **motion**?

- your desk
- a parked car
- a chair rocking
- a dog chasing a ball
- a kite blowing in the wind

Has a **motion** ever made you feel dizzy or sick? If so, what sort of **motion** was it?

encourage

verb

You **encourage** someone if you give praise and support to help the person believe in themselves.

Jill didn't think she could finish the race, but her coach **encouraged** her and she made it!

Which statements would someone make to **encourage** you?

- "You might as well just give up."
- "That's the way to go!"
- "Hang in there!"
- "You can do it."
- "Forget it."

Tell about a time when you weren't sure you could do something, and someone **encouraged** you to try. Who **encouraged** you and what happened?

demand

verb

You **demand** something when you ask firmly for it or order it to be done.

The teacher **demanded** to know who threw the paper airplane.

In which of these statements is someone **demanding** something?

- "Mind me this instant!"
- "Stop that immediately."
- "Am I invited to the party, too?"
- "You must tell me right now."
- "Yes, you may have more ice cream."

How is **demanding** different from nicely asking someone a question? Which do you prefer and why? How do you feel when someone **demands** something of you?

pollution

noun

Pollution dirties the pure air, water, and land of our planet.

Electric and solar-powered cars are good for our planet because they don't create air **pollution**.

Which of the following might cause **pollution**?

- rain
- a rainbow
- exhaust from cars
- oil spilled from a tanker in the ocean
- chemicals from a factory that leak into the ground

What can people do to help stop **pollution**? What are some things that you do?

motion • encourage • demand • pollution

Write on the board the four words studied this week. Read the words with the class and briefly review their meanings. Then conduct the oral activities below.

1 Tell students that you are going to give them a clue about one of the words for the week. They are to find the word that answers the clue.

- When cars burn gasoline, the smoke causes this. **(pollution)**

- Waving your hands and shaking your head are examples of this. **(motion)**

- "Tell me who broke the window!" is an example of someone doing this. **(making a demand)**

- To do this, you might say, "Great job! Keep going!" **(encourage someone)**

2 Read each sentence and ask students to supply the correct word to complete the sentence.

- I ____ you to run. You would be a great class president. **(encourage)**

- When factory owners dump waste into rivers, they cause water ____. **(pollution)**

- I ____ that you return your brother's toy immediately! **(demand)**

- Our dog doesn't like riding in the car, because the ____ makes her carsick. **(motion)**

3 Read each list of words and phrases. Ask students to supply the word that fits best with each.

- movement, rocking, running, dancing **(motion)**

- give someone hope, cheer, applaud **(encourage)**

- dirty water, smoke, gas fumes, smog, industrial waste **(pollution)**

- insist, order, "Do what I tell you to do! Do it now!" **(demand)**

4 Read each sentence and ask students to decide if it is true or false. If the sentence is false, instruct students to explain why.

- Making a demand is a polite way to ask a favor. **(false; when you make a demand, you order someone to do something)**

- Using wind power is one way to cut down on air pollution. **(true)**

- Fans encourage their team by cheering during games. **(true)**

- People often make motions with their hands as they speak. **(true)**

Answers for page 59: 1. C, 2. F, 3. C, 4. J

Name _____

Fill in the bubble next to the correct answer.

1. In which sentence is the word *demand* used correctly?

Ⓐ If it's okay, I demand more potatoes, please.

Ⓑ I demand to get a good night's sleep tonight.

Ⓒ I demand to know who played this trick on me.

Ⓓ You demand to be a firefighter when you grow up, right?

2. *Pollution* ___ our planet's air, water, and land.

Ⓕ dirties

Ⓖ creates

Ⓗ cleans

Ⓙ improves

3. In which sentence is the word *encourage* used correctly?

Ⓐ I encourage you to be quiet immediately!

Ⓑ My parents encourage me to stop bothering my sister.

Ⓒ I encourage you to try out for Saturday's talent show.

Ⓓ Our neighbors encourage us to stay out of their yard.

4. Which sentence tells about *motion*?

Ⓕ We have a large refrigerator in our kitchen.

Ⓖ Our living room has a sofa and two armchairs.

Ⓗ A colorful rug lies on the dining room floor.

Ⓙ A gentle breeze moved the curtains slightly.

Writing

Which do you like better, the gentle, rocking motion of a boat, or the fast, jerky motion of an amusement-park ride? Tell why. Use **motion** in your sentence.

_____

_____

applaud

verb

You **applaud** by clapping your hands to show that you liked something.

The crowd **applauded** when the firefighter brought the child out of the building.

Would you **applaud** for:

- the winner of the school spelling bee?
- your dinner?
- a singer at the end of a song?
- the actors at the end of a play?
- the mail carrier?

Tell about a time when you **applauded** for something. Has anyone ever **applauded** for you? If so, how did you feel?

tattered

adjective

Something is **tattered** if it's old and torn.

Among the things in my great-grandma's trunk in the attic were some **tattered** clothes and antique jewelry.

Which words mean about the same as **tattered**?

- new
- torn
- whole
- ripped
- shredded

Tell about something you and your family have that is **tattered** but is precious anyway. Why is it special?

observe

verb

You **observe** something when you watch or study it carefully.

An astronomer **observes** the stars to learn new information about them.

Which of these mean about the same as **observe**?

- examine
- look at
- plan
- notice
- touch

Which animal would you like to **observe** in order to learn about it? What information would you want to learn?

function

noun

The purpose or job of something is its **function**.

The **function** of the microwave is to cook or heat food.

What is the **function** of a:

- book?
- bicycle?
- teacher?
- newspaper?
- refrigerator?

Do students in your class have any special **functions**? What are they? What about the adults who work at your school? What **functions** do they perform?

applaud • tattered • observe • function

Write on the board the four words studied this week. Read the words with the class and briefly review their meanings. Then conduct the oral activities below.

1 Tell students that you are going to give them a clue about one of the words for the week. They are to find the word that answers the clue.

- You could use this word to describe a raggedy piece of cloth. **(tattered)**

- This is what something does, or what people use it for. **(its function)**

- You might do this to find out more about an animal's habits. **(observe it)**

- You clap your hands when you do this. **(applaud)**

2 Read each sentence and ask students to supply the correct word to complete the sentence.

- At my older sister's party, my ____ was to pass around bowls of snacks. **(function)**

- The homeless man wore old, ____ clothing. **(tattered)**

- Scientists ____ wild animals in their natural habitats. **(observe)**

- Even if I don't enjoy a concert, I usually ____ to be polite. **(applaud)**

3 Read each list of words and phrases. Ask students to supply the word that fits best with each.

- purpose, job, what something is supposed to do **(function)**

- watch carefully, study, examine, pay close attention to **(observe)**

- old, raggedy, torn, full of holes, falling apart **(tattered)**

- clap, cheer, show appreciation and enjoyment **(applaud)**

4 Read each sentence and ask students to decide if it is true or false. If the sentence is false, instruct students to explain why.

- Most brand-new clothing is tattered. **(false; tattered clothing is old and torn)**

- An audience usually applauds when a concert ends. **(true)**

- A table knife's function is to cut food such as meat or to spread food such as butter. **(true)**

- When you observe an animal, you see it for only a moment. **(false; you watch or study it carefully)**

Answers for page 63: 1. C, 2. H, 3. B, 4. F

| **Review Words** | applaud • tattered • observe • function |

Fill in the bubble next to the correct answer.

1. In which sentence is the word *function* used correctly?

Ⓐ Please move that function out of my way.

Ⓑ I bought some tomatoes and a big orange function.

Ⓒ A refrigerator's function is to keep foods cool and fresh.

Ⓓ Carmina's new function is black with red and white stripes.

2. We *applaud* performers to show that we ___ their performance.

Ⓕ disliked

Ⓖ felt bored during

Ⓗ enjoyed

Ⓙ hope they can improve

3. Which word has about the same meaning as *observe*?

Ⓐ help

Ⓑ watch

Ⓒ understand

Ⓓ describe

4. Which word has about the same meaning as *tattered*?

Ⓕ raggedy

Ⓖ striped

Ⓗ fancy

Ⓙ silky

Writing

Pick a useful machine and write about its function. Use **function** in your sentence.

_____

_____

convenient

adjective

Something is **convenient** if it's useful, easy to use, and no trouble.

It's very **convenient** to heat food in a microwave because it's so fast.

Would it be **convenient** if:

- a book you needed was too high to reach?
- someone interrupted you while you were studying?
- the bus you rode stopped right in front of your house?
- the supermarket stayed open twenty-four hours a day?
- your baseball game was at the same time as your brother's?

Tell about something you use at home that's **convenient** for you to reach. Is there something that isn't **convenient** to reach that you need help to get?

postpone

verb

When you **postpone** something, you put it off until later.

We had to **postpone** the picnic until next weekend because of the rain.

Which of the following mean about the same as **postpone**?

- delay
- do now
- reschedule
- begin immediately
- change to another day

Tell about a time when you had to **postpone** something you were planning to do. Why did you have to **postpone** it? Were you able to reschedule it?

discourage

verb

You **discourage** someone if you try to get the person to not do something.

My dad **discouraged** us from climbing the tree because it was too high.

Which statements could you make to **discourage** someone?

- "I don't think that makes much sense."
- "I don't think you should try that."
- "Keep up the good work!"
- "That's not a good idea."
- "Go for it!"

When has someone **discouraged** you from doing something? What was his or her reason? How did you feel?

anxious

adjective

If you are **anxious** to do something, you are waiting eagerly for it to happen.

Kim was **anxious** for the circus to come to town because she loved to watch the trapeze artists.

Would you be **anxious**:

- to catch a bad cold?
- to have your bike stolen?
- for your birthday to come?
- to go to an amusement park?
- for your best friend to spend the night?

Tell about a time when you were **anxious** for something to happen. What were you waiting for? How did you get through the days of waiting?

convenient • postpone • discourage • anxious

Write on the board the four words studied this week. Read the words with the class and briefly review their meanings. Then conduct the oral activities below.

1 Tell students that you are going to give them a clue about one of the words for the week. They are to find the word that answers the clue.

- If you couldn't get to an appointment, you might do this. **(postpone it)**

- Many people feel like this when a holiday is near. **(anxious)**

- If a friend was about to break a school rule, you might try to do this. **(discourage him or her)**

- You might use this word to describe something that works very well for you. **(convenient)**

2 Read each sentence and ask students to supply the correct word to complete the sentence.

- We ____ our dog from chasing the cat by saying, "No!" **(discourage)**

- I was so ____ for my trip to begin that I packed my suitcase a week in advance. **(anxious)**

- Are you sure that this is a ____ time to visit you? **(convenient)**

- Let's ____ the visit until a time that's better for you. **(postpone)**

3 Read each sentence and ask students to tell which word or words are wrong. Then have them provide the correct word from the week's list.

- I'm so unwilling to visit you. I can't wait! **(unwilling/anxious)**

- I'm afraid we'll have to hurry up our meeting. I can't do it today. **(hurry up/postpone)**

- When is a terrible time to phone you? **(terrible/convenient)**

4 Read each sentence and ask students to decide if it is true or false. If the sentence is false, instruct students to explain why.

- We should discourage people from following safety rules. **(false; we should encourage people to follow safety rules)**

- Most kids are anxious for their birthdays to come. **(true)**

- It's convenient to have a lamp right beside your bed. **(true)**

- When you postpone a meeting, you set a later time for it. **(true)**

Answers for page 67: 1. B, 2. J, 3. C, 4. G

| Review Words | convenient • postpone • discourage • anxious |

Fill in the bubble next to the correct answer.

1. Which word has about the same meaning as *postpone*?

Ⓐ hurry

Ⓑ delay

Ⓒ schedule

Ⓓ visit

2. Which word means the opposite of *convenient*?

Ⓕ useful

Ⓖ perfect

Ⓗ enjoyable

Ⓙ troublesome

3. To *discourage* someone from going on a trip, you might ____ .

Ⓐ say that you wish you could go, too

Ⓑ tell that person to have a wonderful time

Ⓒ give reasons why it is not a good idea

Ⓓ help that person pack some clothes

4. If a girl was *anxious* for day camp to start, what might she say?

Ⓕ "I wish it wouldn't start for another month."

Ⓖ "I'm so excited! I can't wait for it to start!"

Ⓗ "It doesn't matter to me when it starts."

Ⓙ "I wish I didn't have to go. I hate camp!"

| Writing |

Which yearly event are you always the most anxious for? Use **anxious** in your sentence.

_____

_____

cooperate

verb

When people work together to do a task, they **cooperate**.

If we all **cooperate**, we can clean up the classroom very quickly.

Which words might be spoken by someone who knows how to **cooperate**?

- "I'll help you with that."
- "Let's do this together."
- "I really don't need you."
- "Please leave me alone."
- "There's room for everyone to help."

What kinds of things do people in your family do to **cooperate** at home? How does this help everyone to get along?

solution

noun

A **solution** is the answer to a question or the explanation of a problem.

The detective found the **solution** to the mystery by studying the clues.

Which of these have a **solution**?

- a riddle
- a puzzle
- your name
- a mystery story
- a phone number

Think of a time when you had a problem. How did you find the **solution**? Have you ever helped someone find the **solution** to his or her problem? How did it make you feel?

knowledge

noun

Knowledge is what you know and what you learn.

My science teacher loves sharing her **knowledge** of nature with us.

What special **knowledge** would you need in order to do the job performed by each of the following workers?

- plumber
- gardener
- teacher
- doctor
- artist

How does the **knowledge** that you get in school help you? How do you think it might help you in the future?

rapid

adjective

Something that's very fast is **rapid**.

My heartbeat became very **rapid** after I ran a mile.

Which words mean about the same as **rapid**?

- slow
- swift
- quick
- speedy
- crawling

Is your breathing **rapid** or slow right now? When does it become **rapid**? How does that feel?

Review

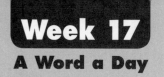

cooperate • solution • knowledge • rapid

Write on the board the four words studied this week. Read the words with the class and briefly review their meanings. Then conduct the oral activities below.

1 Tell students that you are going to give them a clue about one of the words for the week. They are to find the word that answers the clue.

- You could use this word to describe a girl's walk when she is hurrying. **(rapid)**

- This is another word for the explanation to a mystery. **(solution)**

- If you and your friends wanted to build a clubhouse together, you would need to do this. **(cooperate)**

- This is information that people can learn from books or from life experiences. **(knowledge)**

2 Read each sentence and ask students to supply the correct word to complete the sentence.

- I heard ____ footsteps behind me. My sister was hurrying to catch up. **(rapid)**

- If you ____ with me, we can get this done faster. **(cooperate)**

- What is the ____ to this math problem? **(solution)**

- My ____ of dogs is based on living with them. **(knowledge)**

3 Read each sentence and ask students to tell which word is wrong. Then have them provide the correct word from the week's list.

- Terrified, the mouse made a slow escape. **(slow/rapid)**

- I will find the problem to your worries. **(problem/solution)**

- The fastest way to do this job would be to compete with each other. **(compete/cooperate)**

4 Read each sentence and ask students to decide if it is true or false. If the sentence is false, instruct students to explain why.

- All knowledge comes from books. **(false; you can also learn from other people and from life experiences)**

- Family members often cooperate on chores. **(true)**

- Detectives find mysteries in solutions. **(false; they find solutions to mysteries)**

- The most rapid runner usually finishes a race last. **(false; the most rapid runner finishes first)**

Answers for page 71: 1. D, 2. F, 3. C, 4. J

Review Words	cooperate • solution • knowledge • rapid

Fill in the bubble next to the correct answer.

1. Which word has about the same meaning as *rapid*?

Ⓐ plump

Ⓑ thin

Ⓒ slow

Ⓓ quick

2. Which word means the opposite of *solution*?

Ⓕ problem

Ⓖ explanation

Ⓗ detective

Ⓙ answer

3. When people *cooperate* on a project, they ____.

Ⓐ each complete a different project

Ⓑ compete against each other

Ⓒ work together to complete it

Ⓓ fight about ways to complete it

4. How do children gain *knowledge*?

Ⓕ through life experiences

Ⓖ by reading books

Ⓗ by listening to teachers and family members

Ⓙ all of these ways

Writing

Tell about a time when you cooperated with others on a project outside of school. Use **cooperate** in your sentence.

_____

_____

nonsense

noun

Nonsense is something silly that has little or no meaning.

It's **nonsense** to think you can fly if you jump high enough.

Which sentences are **nonsense**?

- Yesterday, I invited an elephant home for lunch.
- The moon is made of green cheese.
- It's important to eat a good breakfast.
- I can hold my breath for three days.
- A baby cat is called a kitten.

What is something that you've heard that you knew was absolute **nonsense**?

Do you ever enjoy **nonsense**? Why or why not?

struggle

verb

When you work hard at something that is difficult, you **struggle**.

I had to **struggle** to learn my spelling words, but now I never misspell them.

Which of these might you do if you **struggle** with something?

- give up
- try harder
- do it over again
- get help from someone
- get it perfect the first time

What do you **struggle** to do well? What is easy for you to do well?

stubborn

adjective

If you are **stubborn**, you like to have things your way and do not like to give in or change.

The **stubborn** child refused to let go of the ball in the toy store.

Which of the following might a **stubborn** person say?

- "I will not go to bed."
- "That's fine; we can try it your way."
- "I don't want vanilla; I only want chocolate."
- "I don't care what you say; it wasn't my fault."
- "You're right; I guess I can change my plans."

Do you know anybody who is **stubborn**? What do you do to get along with that person? Are you ever **stubborn**? About what? Is it ever a good idea to be **stubborn**?

conduct

noun

Your **conduct** is the way you act or behave.

The children's **conduct** at the assembly was so good that they were given extra recess time.

In which of the following places should your **conduct** be calm and quiet?

- in class
- at the park
- in a meeting
- at the library
- at a birthday party

Tell about a time when you got a compliment from a parent, friend, or teacher because of your good **conduct**. What happens if your class's **conduct** is not appropriate?

Review

nonsense • struggle • stubborn • conduct

Write on the board the four words studied this week. Read the words with the class and briefly review their meanings. Then conduct the oral activities below.

1 Tell students that you are going to give them a clue about one of the words for the week. They are to find the word that answers the clue.

- You could use this word to describe a toddler who won't eat her lunch. **(stubborn)**

- Some silly rhymes contain this. **(nonsense)**

- This is another word for *behavior*. **(conduct)**

- This is what you do if math is really hard for you, but you work very hard to get the right answers. **(struggle)**

2 Read each sentence and ask students to supply the correct word to complete the sentence.

- That's ___! There are no space aliens in our school. **(nonsense)**

- Good ___ includes saying please and thank you. **(conduct)**

- My little brother is so ___ that he refuses to wear any other shirt than his red one. **(stubborn)**

- Every day, I ___ to become a better soccer player. **(struggle)**

3 Read each sentence and ask students to tell which word or words are wrong. Then have them provide the correct word from the week's list.

- It is important to me to be a better pitcher, so I will not try to do it. **(not try/struggle)**

- Ana is so willing, she refuses to wear shoes to school. **(willing/stubborn)**

- It's reasonable to say that your family is getting a pet lion. **(reasonable/nonsense)**

4 Read each sentence and ask students to decide if it is true or false. If the sentence is false, instruct students to explain why.

- It is bad conduct to speak with your mouth full. **(true)**

- People must struggle to complete fun, easy jobs. **(false; people must struggle to complete difficult jobs)**

- Nonsense is reasonable. **(false; nonsense is silliness)**

- Stubborn people can be irritating. **(true)**

Answers for page 75: 1. C, 2. J, 3. D, 4. H

A Word a Day • EMC 2793 • © Evan-Moor Corp.

| Review Words | nonsense • struggle • stubborn • conduct |

Fill in the bubble next to the correct answer.

1. Which word has about the same meaning as *conduct*?

Ⓐ schooling

Ⓑ success

Ⓒ behavior

Ⓓ clothing

2. Which word means the opposite of *stubborn*?

Ⓕ beautiful

Ⓖ clever

Ⓗ kind

Ⓙ willing

3. If you must *struggle* to reach a goal, the goal is ___ for you to reach.

Ⓐ very easy

Ⓑ easy

Ⓒ a little hard

Ⓓ quite difficult

4. Which makes sense as a response to *nonsense*?

Ⓕ "That's a wonderful idea! Let's do it!"

Ⓖ "That may be a good idea, but I'm not interested."

Ⓗ "What? That's the silliest thing I ever heard!"

Ⓙ "It makes me very angry to hear you say that."

| Writing |

Write a rule for conduct in your classroom. Use **conduct** in your sentence.

_____

_____

characteristic

noun

A **characteristic** is a trait or a feature that someone or something has.

A long neck is one of the giraffe's most noticeable **characteristics**.

Name a noticeable **characteristic** for each of the following:

- an elephant
- a banana
- a turtle
- snow
- you

What physical **characteristics** do you have that are similar to those of someone else in your family? What personality **characteristics** do you have that are similar?

cherish

verb

When you **cherish** something, it is special to you and you treasure it.

My mother **cherishes** the tea set her mother gave her when she was a little girl.

Which of the following might someone **cherish**?

- old photos of Grandpa as a baby
- Mom's wedding gown
- a sour pickle
- an award
- dust

Tell about something you **cherish**. How did you get it? Why is it so special to you?

expand

verb

When you **expand** something, you make it bigger.

You could see the flat tire **expand** as air was pumped in.

Which of these could you **expand**?

- a brick
- a circle
- a balloon
- a page in a book
- your number of friends

Are you wearing anything that can **expand**? Check around your waist, cuffs, or neck.

edible

adjective

Something that can be eaten is **edible**.

Rhubarb stalks are **edible**, but their leaves can be poisonous.

Which of the following are **edible**?

- mud
- snails
- chicken
- crayons
- strawberries

Can you always tell if plants growing in the wild are **edible**? Do you think it's a good idea to eat things in order to find out?

Review

---

characteristic • cherish • expand • edible

Write on the board the four words studied this week. Read the words with the class and briefly review their meanings. Then conduct the oral activities below.

1 Tell students that you are going to give them a clue about one of the words for the week. They are to find the word that answers the clue.

- You could use this word to describe a wild plant that is safe to eat. **(edible)**

- Intelligence could be one of your teacher's. Patience might be another. **(a characteristic)**

- This is another way to say that you value something very much. **(you cherish it)**

- When you breathe in, you do this to your lungs. **(expand them)**

2 Read each sentence and ask students to supply the correct word to complete the sentence.

- If you eat a big meal, your waistline may _____. **(expand)**

- I will always _____ the ring that my grandma gave me. **(cherish)**

- My favorite _____ of Holly's is her sense of humor. **(characteristic)**

- Don't eat those! That kind of berry is not _____! **(edible)**

3 Read each sentence and ask students to tell which word or words are wrong. Then have them provide the correct word from the week's list.

- To shrink our living space, Dad built another room onto the back of our house. **(shrink/expand)**

- The twins don't care about their great-grandfather's medals from World War II. **(don't care about/cherish)**

- You can eat these wild blackberries. They are poisonous. **(poisonous/edible)**

4 Read each sentence and ask students to decide if it is true or false. If the sentence is false, instruct students to explain why.

- Its black and white fur is a characteristic that helps us recognize the skunk. **(true)**

- Most people cherish their old socks. **(false; most people don't treasure their old socks)**

- When you blow up a balloon, it expands. **(true)**

- Rocks are edible. **(false; you can't eat rocks)**

Answers for page 79: 1. C, 2. F, 3. B, 4. J

Review Words   characteristic • cherish • expand • edible

Fill in the bubble next to the correct answer.

1. **Which word has about the same meaning as *cherish*?**
   Ⓐ dislike
   Ⓑ accompany
   Ⓒ treasure
   Ⓓ excuse

2. **Which word means the opposite of *expand*?**
   Ⓕ shrink
   Ⓖ widen
   Ⓗ stretch
   Ⓙ lengthen

3. **Which might be a girl's *characteristic*?**
   Ⓐ her bicycle
   Ⓑ her shyness
   Ⓒ her brother
   Ⓓ her school

4. **You can ___ something that is *edible*.**
   Ⓕ build a home with
   Ⓖ make clothes from
   Ⓗ read
   Ⓙ eat

Writing

Write about a possession that you cherish. Use **cherish** in your sentence.

_____

_____

destination

noun

The **destination** is the place where someone or something is going.

This year, the **destination** for our family vacation is Hawaii.

Which of the following are **destinations**?

- a sunny beach
- a lakeside cabin
- a bus
- an amusement park
- your bicycle

What is the farthest **destination** you have visited? Did you travel there by train, ship, plane, or car?

landscape

noun

A **landscape** is a painting of natural outdoor scenery.

The art museum had a special exhibit of **landscapes** last spring.

Which of the following might you see in a **landscape**?

- trees
- high-rise buildings
- the ocean
- a freeway
- mountains

Why do you think artists paint **landscapes**? Why do you think people enjoy looking at **landscapes**?

youth

noun

You are a **youth** after childhood and before adulthood.

My grandpa delivered newspapers on his bicycle when he was a **youth**.

Which of these are **youths**?

- your great-aunt
- your grandmother
- your teenaged cousin
- your 16-year-old brother
- your 14-year-old baby sitter

Tell about something your mom or dad did when they were **youths**. How were things different for them than for **youths** today?

verdict

noun

A **verdict** is a decision made by a jury.

The twelve members of the jury discussed the case for hours before reaching a guilty **verdict**.

Which words mean about the same as **verdict**?

- ruling
- finding
- judgment
- argument
- disappointment

Do you think that someday you would like to be part of a jury and help reach a **verdict** in a case?

Review

destination • landscape • youth • verdict

Write on the board the four words studied this week. Read the words with the class and briefly review their meanings. Then conduct the oral activities below.

1 Tell students that you are going to give them a clue about one of the words for the week. They are to find the word that answers the clue.

- This could be "guilty" or "not guilty." (**a verdict**)

- One of these might show some hills and a field. (**a landscape**)

- If you travel somewhere on a train, this is the place where you get off. (**your destination**)

- A teenager is one. (**a youth**)

2 Read each sentence and ask students to supply the correct word to complete the sentence.

- Mr. Goldstein painted a ____ that showed a beach scene. (**landscape**)

- How long do you think it will take the jury to reach its ____? (**verdict**)

- Grandpa was in the high school marching band when he was a ____. (**youth**)

- We finally reached our ____ after six hours on the plane. (**destination**)

3 Read each list of words and phrases. Ask students to supply the word that fits best with each.

- courtroom, jury, decision, guilty or not guilty (**verdict**)

- teenager, high school student, not yet an adult (**youth**)

- painting, outdoor scene, trees, mountains, fields (**landscape**)

- vacation, journey, traveling, the place where you're going (**destination**)

4 Read each sentence and ask students to decide if it is true or false. If the sentence is false, instruct students to explain why.

- You leave from your destination. (**false; your destination is the place where you're going**)

- A verdict tells whether someone did or did not break the law. (**true**)

- A youth is older than 10 and younger than 21. (**true**)

- A landscape is a portrait of a famous person. (**false; a landscape shows outdoor scenery**)

Answers for page 83: 1. D, 2. F, 3. D, 4. H

Review Words   destination • landscape • youth • verdict

Fill in the bubble next to the correct answer.

1. **In a court case, who reaches a *verdict*?**
   - Ⓐ lawyers
   - Ⓑ people who break the law
   - Ⓒ police officers
   - Ⓓ members of the jury

2. **Which phrase means the opposite of *youth*?**
   - Ⓕ senior citizen
   - Ⓖ teenaged boy
   - Ⓗ young woman
   - Ⓙ older child

3. **A *landscape* is a painting that shows ____.**
   - Ⓐ one or more people
   - Ⓑ colorful patterns
   - Ⓒ a bowl of fruit
   - Ⓓ the outdoors

4. **Which question asks about a *destination*?**
   - Ⓕ What book did you borrow from the library?
   - Ⓖ What are we having for dinner tonight?
   - Ⓗ Where are we going on our field trip?
   - Ⓙ Who is your favorite cartoon character?

Writing

If you painted a landscape, what would you put in it? Use **landscape** in your sentence.

_____

_____

theme

noun

A **theme** is the topic or subject of something.

Ana's party had a rainforest **theme**, so all the party favors were rainforest animal toys.

Which of the following could have a **theme**?

- a party
- a book
- a couch
- a movie
- a hairbrush

What was the **theme** of the last book you read?
What **themes** do you find most interesting?

strive

verb

When you **strive**, you make your best effort to do something.

I **strive** to walk a little farther every day on my morning walk.

Which statements would a coach make if he wanted his players to **strive** to play their best game?

- "Give up when it gets hard."
- "Do your best."
- "Try hard."
- "Run away."
- "Make every effort."

What do you **strive** to do well at home? How about in school? What do you **strive** to do in a sport or a hobby?

similar

adjective

Two things are **similar** if they are very much alike.

My brother and I like **similar** sports, but the books we like are totally different.

Which pairs of words name things that are **similar**?

- a basketball and a soccer ball
- a shoe and a slipper
- a radio and a bed
- a piano and a lamp
- a pond and a lake

Tell how you are **similar** to your mom or dad, to a brother or sister, or to your best friend.

thorough

adjective

A **thorough** job is complete and leaves nothing out.

Grace did such a **thorough** job of cleaning that there wasn't a speck of dirt left.

Which of these describe people doing a **thorough** job?

- Anthony stopped doing chores to play ball.
- Ben studied for two hours without a break.
- Without the directions, the boys couldn't complete the model.
- Laurel soon gave up on learning her new piano piece.
- Mom and Josh washed, dried, and put away all the dishes.

Tell about a time when you did a **thorough** job. What were the steps you followed from start to finish? How did you feel afterward? Was there ever a time when you didn't do a **thorough** job? What happened?

theme • strive • similar • thorough

Write on the board the four words studied this week. Read the words with the class and briefly review their meanings. Then conduct the oral activities below.

1 Tell students that you are going to give them a clue about one of the words for the week. They are to find the word that answers the clue.

- This word might describe a well-done, completely finished job. (**thorough**)

- You do this when you try hard to reach a goal. (**strive**)

- A fiction book has at least one, and so does a movie. (**a theme**)

- This word may describe two sisters' looks. (**similar**)

2 Read each sentence and ask students to supply the correct word to complete the sentence.

- Our dog does a _____ job of eating her dinner. She licks the bowl clean. (**thorough**)

- Those two colors are _____. However, one is more reddish than the other. (**similar**)

- Bravery is this story's main _____. (**theme**)

- This year, Ramon will _____ to get better grades than he got last year. (**strive**)

3 Read each sentence and ask students to tell which word or words are wrong. Then have them provide the correct word from the week's list.

- Most twins have completely different looks. (**completely different/similar**)

- I was proud of the sloppy job I did on my school project. (**sloppy/thorough**)

- When I really want something, I don't try to get it. (**don't try/strive**)

4 Read each sentence and ask students to decide if it is true or false. If the sentence is false, instruct students to explain why.

- A children's party might have a fairy-tale theme. (**true**)

- A teacher appreciates it when a student does a thorough job on the homework assignment. (**true**)

- People with similar likes and dislikes are likely to become friends. (**true**)

- Striving is similar to struggling. (**true**)

Answers for page 87: 1. D, 2. F, 3. A, 4. J

Review Words   theme • strive • similar • thorough

Fill in the bubble next to the correct answer.

1. Which word has about the same meaning as *strive*?

Ⓐ wait

Ⓑ hate

Ⓒ like

Ⓓ try

2. Which word means the opposite of *thorough*?

Ⓕ incomplete

Ⓖ brilliant

Ⓗ careful

Ⓙ detailed

3. Which one might be a story's *theme*?

Ⓐ friendship

Ⓑ 32 pages

Ⓒ from the library

Ⓓ fiction

4. An apple is most *similar* to _____ .

Ⓕ a dog

Ⓖ a mountain

Ⓗ the ocean

Ⓙ an orange

Writing

Write about the best birthday party theme that you can think of. Use **theme** in your sentence.

_____

_____

content

adjective

When you are **content**, you are happy and satisfied.

The kitten was so **content** as she sat on my lap that she began to purr.

Which words mean about the same as **content**?

- glad
- upset
- pleased
- dissatisfied
- displeased

What makes you **content**? Do you usually feel **content** or not?

parched

adjective

You are **parched** if you are extremely hot and dry and need water.

We ran out of bottled water and were totally **parched** by the time we had driven across the desert.

Which of these mean about the same as **parched**?

- moist
- damp
- dried out
- thirsty
- dehydrated

Tell about a time when you were **parched**. What did you do? What happens to plants when they're **parched**?

qualify

verb

You **qualify** when you reach a level of skill or knowledge that allows you to do something.

Our team had to win three games in order to **qualify** to go to the finals.

Which activities would you need to **qualify** for?

- making your bed
- teaching in an elementary school
- joining the young people's orchestra
- competing as a gymnast in the Olympics
- representing your school at a statewide spelling bee

Imagine that you are offering to walk your neighbor's dog. What would you say to convince him or her that you **qualify** to do this job?

quench

verb

When you **quench** your thirst, you drink until you are no longer thirsty.

On a hot summer's day, there's nothing like ice-cold lemonade to **quench** my thirst.

In which of these situations might you need to **quench** your thirst?

- while you're sleeping
- after eating salty chips
- after running a long race
- when working out in the garden
- sitting on the beach under a hot sun

What is your favorite beverage to drink when you need to **quench** your thirst?

content • parched • qualify • quench

Write on the board the four words studied this week. Read the words with the class and briefly review their meanings. Then conduct the oral activities below.

1 Tell students that you are going to give them a clue about one of the words for the week. They are to find the word that answers the clue.

- This word describes a plant that no one has watered for a month. **(parched)**

- You do this if you have the skills to do a particular job. **(qualify for the job)**

- This word describes someone who has everything he or she wants. **(content)**

- A large glass of water will do this to your thirst. **(quench it)**

2 Read each sentence and ask students to supply the correct word to complete the sentence.

- Players don't ____ for the basketball team unless they earn good grades. **(qualify)**

- It had not rained all summer, and the farmer's crops were ____. **(parched)**

- A long-distance runner will need to ____ his thirst at the end of the race. **(quench)**

- I feel ____ when I'm with my family and friends. **(content)**

3 Read each sentence and ask students to tell which word or words are wrong. Then have them provide the correct word from the week's list.

- A dry summer left the crops green and moist. **(green and moist/parched)**

- When she purrs, my cat seems unhappy. **(unhappy/content)**

- Congratulations! You didn't meet the requirements for the team! **(didn't meet the requirements/qualify)**

4 Read each sentence and ask students to decide if it is true or false. If the sentence is false, instruct students to explain why.

- Water will quench animals' thirst. **(true)**

- People are grouchy when they feel content. **(false; they are happy and satisfied)**

- When you are parched, you feel very thirsty. **(true)**

- Most high school graduates with good grades qualify for college. **(true)**

Answers for page 91: 1. B, 2. J, 3. B, 4. H

| **Review Words** | content • parched • qualify • quench |

Fill in the bubble next to the correct answer.

1. Which word has about the same meaning as *parched*?

Ⓐ moist

Ⓑ dry

Ⓒ raggedy

Ⓓ wrinkled

2. Which word means the opposite of *content*?

Ⓕ alert

Ⓖ mean

Ⓗ intelligent

Ⓙ dissatisfied

3. Who would *qualify* for a high school teaching job?

Ⓐ a high school student

Ⓑ a college graduate

Ⓒ a fifth grader

Ⓓ a middle school student

4. Water, milk, and juice *quench* my ____.

Ⓕ hunger

Ⓖ tiredness

Ⓗ thirst

Ⓙ curiosity

Writing

Write about a job that you would like to have. Tell what you would need to do to qualify for it. Use **qualify** in your sentence.

_____

_____

opponent

noun

An **opponent** is someone who is trying to beat you in a contest or an election.

Sue's **opponent** in the tennis match scored the last point and won the trophy.

Which of the following could be **opponents**?

- the person you're trying to beat at checkers
- the person you're working with on a class project
- the person running against you for class president
- the person who is teaching you how to play the piano
- the person who's trying to kick the ball into the goal that you're defending

What would you do to show your **opponent** that you are a good sport?

opportunity

noun

An **opportunity** is a chance to do something.

My dad has the **opportunity** to get a great new job, so we might have to move.

Which of the following offer you an **opportunity**?

- drinking a glass of water
- being chosen to go to science camp
- getting an invitation to a birthday party
- putting your dirty clothes in the laundry basket
- receiving an offer to try out for the school play

What special **opportunity** has been made available to you? Did you take advantage of that **opportunity**? What happened?

advise

verb

When you **advise** someone, you give suggestions that will help him or her to make a decision.

Jamie **advised** me to buy the red shirt because it went better with my jacket.

What would you **advise** a friend who:

- lost a dollar on the playground?
- accidentally broke his or her mom's vase?
- wanted to play ball with you but had chores to do?
- wanted to buy a new toy but didn't have enough money?
- was afraid to tell the teacher about losing a book?

Tell about a time when you **advised** someone about something, or a time when someone **advised** you. How did it turn out?

positive

adjective

You're **positive** about something when you are absolutely certain of it.

I'm **positive** I left my coat on the playground, because I took it off to swing on the bars.

Which statements show that the speaker is **positive** about something?

- "I'm not sure."
- "I know that for a fact."
- "I have no doubt about it."
- "I really haven't made up my mind yet."
- "I give you my word that you can count on me."

What is something that you are absolutely **positive** about? How do you know for sure?

opponent • opportunity • advise • positive

Write on the board the four words studied this week. Read the words with the class and briefly review their meanings. Then conduct the oral activities below.

1 Tell students that you are going to give them a clue about one of the words for the week. They are to find the word that answers the clue.

- When you feel this way, you are absolutely sure. **(positive)**

- You might do this if a friend asked for help with a decision. **(advise him or her)**

- If you get one of these, you have a chance. **(an opportunity)**

- In a race, this is someone who's competing against you. **(an opponent)**

2 Read each sentence and ask students to supply the correct word to complete the sentence.

- I ____ you not to break school rules. **(advise)**

- Last summer, my family had an ____ to visit a national park. **(opportunity)**

- Will you be my ____ in a game of Scrabble? **(opponent)**

- I'm ____ that my dog loves me. **(positive)**

3 Read each sentence and ask students to tell which word is wrong. Then have them provide the correct word from the week's list.

- My cousin had the misfortune to get into a top university. **(misfortune/opportunity)**

- I'm absolutely sure that I'm right; in fact, I'm uncertain. **(uncertain/positive)**

- Taylor beat almost every teammate in the gymnastics competition. **(teammate/opponent)**

4 Read each sentence and ask students to decide if it is true or false. If the sentence is false, instruct students to explain why.

- It is best not to advise people who don't ask for your suggestions. **(true)**

- People should always ignore opportunities. **(false; an opportunity is a chance to do or get something; usually something good)**

- When you are positive about something, you are sure. **(true)**

- Opponents play against you in ballgames. **(true)**

Answers for page 95: 1. D, 2. F, 3. B, 4. G

Name _____

Fill in the bubble next to the correct answer.

1. Which word has about the same meaning as *opportunity*?

Ⓐ misfortune

Ⓑ situation

Ⓒ event

Ⓓ chance

2. Which word means the opposite of *positive*?

Ⓕ uncertain

Ⓖ sure

Ⓗ convinced

Ⓙ excited

3. Which sentence tells about someone who *advises* someone else?

Ⓐ My friend and I sometimes quarrel with each other.

Ⓑ My sister helps me decide which books to read.

Ⓒ My cousin and I play on the same soccer team.

Ⓓ My grandpa sometimes bakes cookies for us.

4. In a soccer game, your *opponent* is someone who is ___.

Ⓕ on your team

Ⓖ playing against you

Ⓗ selling refreshments

Ⓙ coaching your team

Writing

Write about a time when a family member advised you to do, or not to do, something. Use **advise** in your sentence.

_____

_____

peer

noun

A person who is in your age group is a **peer**.

Mario worked with a group of his **peers** to clean up the school garden.

Which ones could be your **peer**?

- your dentist
- your best friend
- the school secretary
- the child sitting next to you in class
- another player on your baseball team

Tell about a time when you and a **peer** helped each other or worked on a project together. Do you enjoy working with a **peer**? Why or why not?

satisfactory

adjective

Something that is good enough is **satisfactory**.

Her first book report was **satisfactory**, but the next one she wrote was outstanding.

Which of the following mean about the same as **satisfactory**?

- okay
- passing
- acceptable
- outstanding
- unacceptable

Tell about a time when you did something that was **satisfactory**, but the next time you improved and did an outstanding job.

respond

verb

When you answer or reply, you **respond**.

The invitation said to **respond** by phone if you planned to attend the party.

How would you **respond** if:

- your mother asked if you wanted more dessert?
- your best friend wanted you to come over and play?
- your brother asked if he could borrow your favorite toy?
- someone called to talk to your dad, but he was at work?
- your teacher asked for a volunteer to take a note to the office?

Have you ever had to **respond** to an invitation? Did you **respond** by phone, in writing, or in person? What is a polite way to **respond** if you cannot accept an invitation?

request

verb

When you **request** something, you ask for it politely.

Margo called the radio station to **request** that they play her favorite song, and they did!

How would you **request** each of the following?

- a drink of water
- to join in a ballgame
- another helping of potatoes
- to watch your favorite TV show
- to have your teacher repeat the directions

What have you had to **request** at school? What words can you use to **request** politely?

peer • satisfactory • respond • request

Write on the board the four words studied this week. Read the words with the class and briefly review their meanings. Then conduct the oral activities below.

1 Tell students that you are going to give them a clue about one of the words for the week. They are to find the word that answers the clue.

- This word describes grades that are okay but not great. (**satisfactory**)

- You might do this if you wanted someone to do you a favor. (**request the favor**)

- You might do this if you received an invitation. (**respond to it**)

- Your best friend is one if he or she is about your age. (**a peer**)

2 Read each sentence and ask students to supply the correct word to complete the sentence.

- My mom and I like the same music, even though she is not my ___. (**peer**)

- I'd like to ___ that you be a little quieter. (**request**)

- I wonder how Dad will ___ if I ask for a new bike. (**respond**)

- Jenny does ___ work in spelling, but her math work is truly excellent. (**satisfactory**)

3 Read each sentence and ask students to tell which word or words are wrong. Then have them provide the correct word from the week's list.

- If you do an unacceptable job on your work, you will get an okay grade. (**an unacceptable/a satisfactory**)

- The third-grade boys play after-school soccer with a group of adults from another school. (**adults/peers**)

- The answering machine voice said, "Leave your name and number and we'll question right away." (**question/respond**)

- I'd like to answer that you return my sweater right away. (**answer/request**)

4 Read each sentence and ask students to decide if it is true or false. If the sentence is false, instruct students to explain why.

- It is polite to respond to an invitation. (**true**)

- Your peer is about twice your age. (**false; your peer is in your age group**)

- A satisfactory musical performance is all right but not excellent. (**true**)

- Requesting a favor is the same as doing a favor for someone. (**false; to request means to ask**)

Answers for page 99: 1. B, 2. F, 3. C, 4. G

Review Words   peer • satisfactory • respond • request

Fill in the bubble next to the correct answer.

1. Which word has about the same meaning as *request*?
- Ⓐ answer
- Ⓑ ask
- Ⓒ suggest
- Ⓓ advise

2. Which word means the opposite of *satisfactory*?
- Ⓕ unacceptable
- Ⓖ okay
- Ⓗ fine
- Ⓙ passable

3. Which sentence tells about someone who *responds* to someone else?
- Ⓐ I sent Shelby an invitation to my birthday party.
- Ⓑ I phoned to ask if Grandma could bake a cake for me.
- Ⓒ Shelby replied that she would love to come.
- Ⓓ Grandma bakes cakes with colorful decorations.

4. Your *peer* is someone who is ____.
- Ⓕ your baby brother or sister
- Ⓖ about the same age as you are
- Ⓗ about ten years older than you are
- Ⓙ your grandparent, aunt, or uncle

Writing

Write about something you requested in the past. Use **request** in your sentence.

_____

_____

disaster

noun

A **disaster** is something that causes much damage or loss.

It was a **disaster** when the tornado destroyed all the buildings on the main street of town.

Which of these are **disasters**?

- a train wreck
- walking a dog
- children singing
- a town being flooded
- buildings falling during an earthquake

Explain how keeping canned foods, water, flashlights, a radio, batteries, and blankets in your house can help you be prepared for a **disaster**.

hardship

noun

A **hardship** is a difficult situation.

The first settlers in America faced many **hardships**, including illness and hunger.

Which of the following mean about the same as **hardship**?

- difficulty
- surprise
- suffering
- misfortune
- happiness

What other **hardships** do people sometimes have to face?

headquarters

noun

Headquarters is the main office where members of a group meet and decisions are made.

The police officer called **headquarters** to request help from more officers.

Which of the following groups might have **headquarters**?

- babies
- firefighters
- forest rangers
- Girl Scouts or Boy Scouts
- cartoon characters

If you were going to form a neighborhood club, where would its **headquarters** be?

reserve

verb

If you arrange to have something held so that you may use it at a later time, you **reserve** it.

We will call the restaurant to **reserve** a table for dinner tonight.

Which of these could you **reserve**?

- the gas pump at the station
- a place at a summer camp
- a seat on an airplane
- a seat at a ballgame
- the bell at school

Why is it a good idea to **reserve** things, such as a seat on an airplane or a hotel room, ahead of time?

disaster • hardship • headquarters • reserve

Write on the board the four words studied this week. Read the words with the class and briefly review their meanings. Then conduct the oral activities below.

1 Tell students that you are going to give them a clue about one of the words for the week. They are to find the word that answers the clue.

- An army, the police department, or a business may have one of these. **(headquarters)**

- You do this when you call a restaurant and ask them to save you a table. **(reserve it)**

- This situation is difficult to deal with, but it isn't quite as bad as a disaster. **(a hardship)**

- These include fires, floods, and earthquakes. **(disasters)**

2 Read each sentence and ask students to supply the correct word to complete the sentence.

- Victims of a _____ may receive help from the government or a charity. **(disaster)**

- I want to _____ some tickets for the baseball game. **(reserve)**

- Officers took the lost child to police _____. **(headquarters)**

- It is a _____ for city residents when our electrical power fails. **(hardship)**

3 Read each list of words and phrases. Ask students to supply the word that fits best with each.

- main office, army, police, company **(headquarters)**

- earthquake, hurricane, car wreck, forest fire **(disaster)**

- job loss, illness, difficulty, power failure **(hardship)**

- save for later, restaurant table, concert tickets, airplane seats **(reserve)**

4 Read each sentence and ask students to decide if it is true or false. If the sentence is false, instruct students to explain why.

- Not being able to get your car fixed would be a hardship. **(true)**

- A light rainstorm is a disaster. **(false; a disaster causes more damage than a light rainstorm)**

- To get a good seat at a concert, you should reserve ahead of time. **(true)**

- A company's president might work at the company's headquarters. **(true)**

Answers for page 103: 1. C, 2. F, 3. D, 4. J

Review Words **Review Words** | disaster • hardship • headquarters • reserve

Fill in the bubble next to the correct answer.

1. Which sentence tells about a *hardship*?

Ⓐ My grandparents went on a trip to Alaska.

Ⓑ Grandma gets up around 7:30 in the morning.

Ⓒ During the 1980s, my grandpa lost his job.

Ⓓ Grandpa was a carpenter in Los Angeles.

2. Which phrase means the opposite of *disaster*?

Ⓕ fortunate event

Ⓖ normal routine

Ⓗ puzzling situation

Ⓙ terrible tragedy

3. To *reserve* a seat on a plane means to ____.

Ⓐ sit in it

Ⓑ give it to someone who needs it

Ⓒ repair it

Ⓓ arrange to use it in the future

4. A company's *headquarters* is its ____.

Ⓕ president

Ⓖ location

Ⓗ main product

Ⓙ main office

Writing

Write about something you'd like to reserve for future use. Use **reserve** in your sentence.

_____

_____

route

noun

The path you take to get somewhere is the **route**.

The road was blocked, so we had to take another **route** to get to school.

Which of the following mean about the same as **route**?

- way
- map
- road
- street
- distance

Describe the shortest **route** from our classroom to the office. Now can you describe a different **route**?

surface

noun

The **surface** is the outer layer of something.

Before you paint a picture, cover the top of your desk with newspaper to keep the **surface** clean.

Which of the following are on the **surface**?

- the roots of a plant
- the seeds of an apple
- an underground tunnel
- butter on a slice of toast
- grass growing in the ground

How is the **surface** of a peach different from the **surface** of an apple?

task

noun

A **task** is a small job or chore.

My sister's **task** every night is to set the table for dinner.

Which of the following are **tasks**?

- washing the car
- watching a movie
- mowing the lawn
- playing basketball
- sweeping the garage floor

Tell about the **tasks** you do at home. How often do you do them? Which is your favorite **task**? Which **task** is your least favorite?

announce

verb

When you **announce** something, you make it known to the public.

The birth of my little sister was **announced** in our local paper.

Which of these might be **announced** on TV or the radio?

- the winner of the Best Movie of the Year award
- the score of the football game
- the weather for tomorrow
- the time you go to bed
- your phone number

Tell about a time when you or someone in your family had good news to **announce**.

route • surface • task • announce

Write on the board the four words studied this week. Read the words with the class and briefly review their meanings. Then conduct the oral activities below.

1 Tell students that you are going to give them a clue about one of the words for the week. They are to find the word that answers the clue.

- Drying the dishes is one. **(a task)**

- People often do this after they decide to get married. **(announce it)**

- You take one of these each time you travel from one place to another. **(a route)**

- Sandpaper has a rough one. Glass has a smooth one. **(surface)**

2 Read each sentence and ask students to supply the correct word to complete the sentence.

- Ladies and gentlemen, we wish to _____ that the show will begin in 10 minutes. **(announce)**

- Walking the dog is my daily _____. **(task)**

- An apple has a smooth, often shiny _____. **(surface)**

- I take the shortest _____ from my house to my friend Noah's place. **(route)**

3 Read each list of words and phrases. Ask students to supply the word that fits best with each.

- job, chore, washing the dishes, taking out the trash **(task)**

- skin, covering, crust, outer layer **(surface)**

- make a public statement, say officially, declare **(announce)**

- path, road, shortcut, the way to go **(route)**

4 Read each sentence and ask students to decide if it is true or false. If the sentence is false, instruct students to explain why.

- Every journey has a route. **(true)**

- When you announce an event, you keep it a secret. **(false; when you announce an event, you tell about it in public)**

- Having brown hair is a task. **(false; a task is a job or a chore)**

- A peach has a large seed called a "pit" on its surface. **(false; a pit is in the very middle of a peach, under its surface)**

Answers for page 107: 1. A, 2. H, 3. B, 4. H

Name _____

Fill in the bubble next to the correct answer.

1. Which word has about the same meaning as *task*?

Ⓐ chore

Ⓑ journey

Ⓒ conversation

Ⓓ test

2. Which word means the opposite of *surface*?

Ⓕ skin

Ⓖ top

Ⓗ inside

Ⓙ tail

3. To *announce* an event means to tell about it ___.

Ⓐ privately

Ⓑ publicly

Ⓒ in a book

Ⓓ quietly

4. Mom's *route* to work is ___.

Ⓕ a skill she needs in order to do her job

Ⓖ a special uniform that she wears to work

Ⓗ the way she goes as she travels to work

Ⓙ the kind of computer she uses at work

Writing

Write about the route you usually take from home to a friend's place. Use **route** in your sentence.

_____

_____

praise

noun

Words that express approval or admiration are **praise**.

The teacher was full of **praise** for her class because of their great singing performance at the school concert.

Which of the following statements are examples of giving **praise**?

- "Great job!"
- "Let me help you."
- "That's excellent work!"
- "I think you're going to need to try that again."
- "I love the bright colors you used in that picture!"

Tell about a time when someone gave you a lot of **praise** for something. What was it for? How did the **praise** make you feel about the job you did?

admire

verb

If you respect and look up to someone, you **admire** him or her.

I **admire** people who can play a musical instrument.

Which words mean about the same as **admire**?

- honor
- ignore
- interrupt
- appreciate
- understand

Tell about someone who you **admire**. Why do you **admire** that person? What would you like to be **admired** for someday?

ponder

verb

You **ponder** something when you think about it carefully.

Scientists **ponder** the existence of life on other planets, but no one has proven it yet.

Which of these mean about the same as **ponder**?

- study
- refuse
- accept
- examine
- consider

What is something you have **pondered**? Did you find an answer?

restrain

verb

When you prevent someone from doing something, you **restrain** him or her.

Joe had to **restrain** his dog so it wouldn't take off and chase the neighbor's cat.

Which of the following mean about the same as **restrain**?

- let go
- control
- set free
- hold back
- take control of

Have you ever had to **restrain** someone or something? What did you keep the person from doing? How did you **restrain** the person? Have you ever had to **restrain** yourself?

praise • admire • ponder • restrain

Write on the board the four words studied this week. Read the words with the class and briefly review their meanings. Then conduct the oral activities below.

1 Tell students that you are going to give them a clue about one of the words for the week. They are to find the word that answers the clue.

- Zoos use cages to do this to wild animals. **(restrain them)**

- You might do this when you have an important decision to make. **(ponder)**

- This shows approval and makes people feel good. **(praise)**

- If you look up to someone, you feel this way about that person. **(you admire him or her)**

2 Read each sentence and ask students to supply the correct word to complete the sentence.

- I know you are mad, but please try to ____ your temper. **(restrain)**

- I ____ my mom's patience and kindness. **(admire)**

- Listening to my family's ____ of my project made me feel proud of myself. **(praise)**

- Let's take some time to ____ this important question. **(ponder)**

3 Read each sentence and ask students to tell which word is wrong. Then have them provide the correct word from the week's list.

- I love to receive criticism such as "Good job!" and "Way to go!" **(criticism/praise)**

- I had to release my baby brother so he wouldn't tear my library book. **(release/restrain)**

- You're great! I disrespect you a lot! **(disrespect/admire)**

4 Read each sentence and ask students to decide if it is true or false. If the sentence is false, instruct students to explain why.

- Ranchers put fences around pastures to restrain the cows. **(true)**

- Many people admire rock stars and movie actors. **(true)**

- "Boo!" and "You're terrible!" are examples of praise. **(false; they are examples of criticism)**

- When you ponder an idea, you think about it carefully. **(true)**

Answers for page 111: 1. C, 2. J, 3. B, 4. G

Review Words praise • admire • ponder • restrain

Fill in the bubble next to the correct answer.

1. **What do you do when you *ponder*?**
   Ⓐ go from place to place
   Ⓑ shop at a store
   Ⓒ think about something
   Ⓓ teach someone how to do something

2. **Which word means the opposite of *admire*?**
   Ⓕ need
   Ⓖ treasure
   Ⓗ love
   Ⓙ disrespect

3. **Which sentence tells about someone who *restrains* an animal?**
   Ⓐ I let my dog into the backyard so she could chase her ball.
   Ⓑ I grabbed my dog's collar so she wouldn't run into the street.
   Ⓒ I like it when my cat sleeps on my bed with me.
   Ⓓ I set the cat's food on a table so the dog couldn't reach it.

4. **You give someone *praise* to show that you ___.**
   Ⓕ feel sorry for that person
   Ⓖ think that person has done well
   Ⓗ believe that person can improve
   Ⓙ dislike that person's behavior

Writing

Write about someone you know who deserves praise. Use **praise** in your sentence.

_____

_____

zest

noun

When you have **zest**, you show enjoyment and enthusiasm.

The clowns performed with such **zest** that the crowd got excited, too.

Which words describe someone with **zest**?

- lively
- sleepy
- active
- bored
- enthusiastic

Do you know someone who is full of **zest**? What is that person like?

doze

verb

When you **doze**, you fall into a light sleep for a short time.

The movie was so boring that I started to **doze** off.

Which of these mean about the same as **doze**?

- nap
- study
- snooze
- awaken
- slumber

Where is your favorite place to **doze** on a lazy day?

A Word a Day • EMC 2793 • © Evan-Moor Corp.

hesitate

verb

If you pause for a short time before you do something, you **hesitate**.

Bud **hesitated** a minute before jumping into the cold lake.

If you **hesitated**, would you:

- be the first one to answer the question?
- stand for a moment at the corner before crossing?
- want to be at the front of the line to ride the roller coaster?
- wait a few days before going to meet the new neighbors?
- ask your friend to try the strange-looking food before you tasted it?

Tell about a time when you **hesitated** before doing something. What made you pause? Did you finally go ahead and do it?

optimistic

adjective

An **optimistic** person always believes that things will turn out well.

Even though Jay had a broken arm, he was **optimistic** that it would heal in time for baseball season.

Which statements would an **optimistic** person make?

- "I always have the worst luck."
- "Everything's going to be fine!"
- "Nothing ever works out for me."
- "Tomorrow will be a better day."
- "I know I'm going to feel much better soon!"

Do you know an **optimistic** person? What is he or she like? Do you like being around someone who's **optimistic**? Why or why not?

zest • doze • hesitate • optimistic

Write on the board the four words studied this week. Read the words with the class and briefly review their meanings. Then conduct the oral activities below.

1 Tell students that you are going to give them a clue about one of the words for the week. They are to find the word that answers the clue.

- This word describes someone who expects good things to happen. **(optimistic)**

- You might do this before making a decision when you're unsure. **(hesitate)**

- You might do this if you were reading a boring book in a comfortable chair. **(doze off)**

- You have this when you feel enthusiastic and joyful. **(zest)**

2 Read each sentence and ask students to supply the correct word to complete the sentence.

- Please help yourself to dessert; don't _____. **(hesitate)**

- I often _____ off on the bus ride home from day camp. **(doze)**

- Mayzie is an _____ person, so she thinks we are sure to win the talent show. **(optimistic)**

- Dad loves to cook, so he cooks with _____. **(zest)**

3 Read each sentence and ask students to tell which word or words are wrong. Then have them provide the correct word from the week's list.

- I feel hopeless about moving—I'm sure that our new home will be great! **(hopeless/optimistic)**

- It is smart to act immediately before making an important decision. **(act immediately/hesitate)**

- I just love Italian food, so I eat it with boredom! **(boredom/zest)**

4 Read each sentence and ask students to decide if it is true or false. If the sentence is false, instruct students to explain why.

- People sometimes doze off when they feel bored. **(true)**

- A baseball player who hesitates may not catch the ball. **(true)**

- This is an optimistic statement: "I just know that I'm going to fail the test." **(false; an optimistic person believes that things will turn out well)**

- *Zest* is another word for *weariness*. **(false; zest means enthusiasm)**

Answers for page 115: 1. A, 2. J, 3. C, 4. G

Review Words	zest • doze • hesitate • optimistic

Fill in the bubble next to the correct answer.

1. Which word has about the same meaning as *hesitate*?

Ⓐ pause

Ⓑ hurry

Ⓒ stroll

Ⓓ race

2. Which word means the opposite of *optimistic*?

Ⓕ enthusiastic

Ⓖ cooperative

Ⓗ interested

Ⓙ negative

3. When would you be most likely to *doze* off?

Ⓐ during a conversation with a good friend

Ⓑ during breakfast on a Saturday morning

Ⓒ while watching TV after playing sports all day

Ⓓ while waiting for your birthday party to start

4. Lani draws with *zest* because she ____.

Ⓕ feels bored

Ⓖ loves to draw

Ⓗ isn't a good artist

Ⓙ doesn't like to draw

Writing

Write about a time when it was best to hesitate. Use **hesitate** in your sentence.

_____

_____

mechanic

noun

A **mechanic** knows all about how machines work and can repair them.

When our car wouldn't start, we took it to a **mechanic**, who soon got it running again.

Which of the following might a **mechanic** do?

- fix your sink
- fix an oil leak
- give an engine a tuneup
- repair your computer
- replace the car battery

Would you like to be a **mechanic**? Why or why not?

recreation

noun

Activities that people do in their free time are called **recreation**.

For **recreation**, my dad likes to play tennis on his days off work.

Which activities would a person do for **recreation**?

- go bowling
- mow the lawn
- collect stamps
- play a board game
- clean the bathroom

Tell about the activities the people in your family do for **recreation**. What things do you do together for **recreation**?

nourishment

noun

Nourishment is the food that a person, animal, or plant needs to stay healthy.

The newborn puppies got their **nourishment** from their mother's milk.

What would provide **nourishment** for:

- you?
- a cat?
- a plant?
- a horse?
- a newborn baby?

Imagine that you're an athlete getting ready to run a big race. What kinds of foods do you think would give you the **nourishment** you need?

persuade

verb

You **persuade** someone when you give him or her reason to do as you say.

Janie **persuaded** me to choose fruit for dessert because it's healthier than cake.

What would you say to **persuade**:

- your brother to turn down his music?
- your parents to let you stay up later?
- your best friend to loan you a game?
- your sister to take your turn doing the dishes?
- your teacher to give you an extra day to do an assignment?

Tell about a time when someone **persuaded** you to do something other than what you had planned. How did it turn out?

mechanic • recreation • nourishment • persuade

Write on the board the four words studied this week. Read the words with the class and briefly review their meanings. Then conduct the oral activities below.

1 Tell students that you are going to give them a clue about one of the words for the week. They are to find the word that answers the clue.

- You need this to build a strong, healthy body. **(nourishment)**

- This includes sports, hobbies, and games. **(recreation)**

- You do this when you convince someone to change his or her mind. **(persuade that person)**

- This is someone who repairs cars or other machinery. **(a mechanic)**

2 Read each sentence and ask students to supply the correct word to complete the sentence.

- How can I _____ you to trade your muffin for my apple? **(persuade)**

- Hospital patients need good _____ to help them get well. **(nourishment)**

- The airplane _____ replaced a broken part in the jet engine. **(mechanic)**

- My family plays board games for _____. **(recreation)**

3 Read each list of words and phrases. Ask students to supply the word that fits best with each.

- list reasons why, talk into, convince **(persuade)**

- tunes engines, fixes machinery, repairs cars **(mechanic)**

- free-time activities, swimming, biking, sports **(recreation)**

- food, milk, builds strong bodies, healthful **(nourishment)**

4 Read each sentence and ask students to decide if it is true or false. If the sentence is false, instruct students to explain why.

- Persuading someone to do something is the same as ordering that person to do it. **(false; persuasion involves explaining why your way is the best way to go)**

- Food provides nourishment. **(true)**

- A mechanic knows how to build or repair an engine. **(true)**

- Doing homework is a form of recreation. **(false; most students do not do homework in their free time)**

Answers for page 119: 1. C, 2. F, 3. B, 4. J

Review Words	mechanic • recreation • nourishment • persuade

Fill in the bubble next to the correct answer.

1. From which of these does a plant get *nourishment*?

Ⓐ wild birds
Ⓑ garden paths
Ⓒ the soil
Ⓓ garden clippers

2. Which word means the opposite of *recreation*?

Ⓕ work
Ⓖ swimming
Ⓗ fun
Ⓙ sunbathing

3. A *mechanic* is a person who ___.

Ⓐ makes artwork
Ⓑ repairs engines
Ⓒ cooks restaurant meals
Ⓓ writes books

4. Which word has about the same meaning as *persuade*?

Ⓕ teach
Ⓖ explain
Ⓗ demand
Ⓙ convince

Writing

Write about a park that you like. Tell what people can do there. Use **recreation** in your sentence.

_____

_____

include

verb

When you make something part of something else, you **include** it.

I plan to **include** all my classmates in my birthday celebration.

Which of the following are examples of **including**?

- needing to buy batteries for your remote-controlled car
- inviting a friend to work on your group's project
- leaving someone out because you don't like him or her
- getting breakfast when you pay for the hotel room
- adding names to the guest list

What books would be **included** on your list of "best reads"? What might be **included** on a breakfast menu at a restaurant?

insist

verb

You **insist** when you make a demand about something and won't change your mind.

Katie **insisted** on hiking in a dress even though her mother suggested she wear jeans.

Which of the following would someone say to **insist** about something?

- "It's really completely up to you."
- "I won't take no for an answer."
- "You absolutely must do it right now."
- "Go ahead and do whatever you choose."
- "You don't have a choice; you have to go."

Tell about a time when someone **insisted** that you do something. How did it make you feel? What is something that you have **insisted** on? Did you get your way?

creative

adjective

A **creative** person uses his or her imagination to come up with new ideas.

My **creative** brother should be a writer, since he is always thinking up wild stories.

Which of these words mean about the same as **creative**?

- dull
- artistic
- talented
- ordinary
- imaginative

In what ways do you like to be **creative**? Do you like to sing, dance, paint, write, play an instrument, or invent things?

flexible

adjective

If you are **flexible**, you are willing and able to make changes.

Dad can pick us up after school because his schedule is **flexible**.

Which of the following might a **flexible** person say?

- "I can readjust my plans so that everything will work out."
- "I'm open to going to the movies or to play miniature golf."
- "The only flavor I want is chocolate."
- "No, I only want to do it my way."
- "Either way is fine with me."

Tell about a time when you were **flexible** and willing to change something you were doing or wanted to do. Why is it important to be **flexible** sometimes?

include • insist • creative • flexible

Write on the board the four words studied this week. Read the words with the class and briefly review their meanings. Then conduct the oral activities below.

1 Tell students that you are going to give them a clue about one of the words for the week. They are to find the word that answers the clue.

- This word describes people who are willing to change their plans. **(flexible)**

- When you do this, you won't take no for an answer. **(insist)**

- This word describes artists and songwriters. **(creative)**

- When you bring someone new into a group, you do this.
  (you include him or her)

2 Read each sentence and ask students to supply the correct word to complete the sentence.

- Thanks for being ___ enough to change your plans at the last minute. **(flexible)**

- We ___ that you stay for dinner. **(insist)**

- Let's ___ the Pine family in our picnic plans. **(include)**

- Bo is a ___ cook who likes to invent new recipes. **(creative)**

3 Read each sentence and ask students to tell which word or words are wrong. Then have them provide the correct word from the week's list.

- Thanks for changing your mind and seeing things our way—you're always so stubborn! **(stubborn/flexible)**

- I absolutely hope that you sit down and be quiet right NOW! **(hope/insist)**

- What a fantastic story! You are so unimaginative.
  (unimaginative/creative)

- Let's leave out that wonderful family the next time we have a party.
  (leave out/include)

4 Read each sentence and ask students to decide if it is true or false. If the sentence is false, instruct students to explain why.

- A creative artist copies other artists' work. **(false; he or she comes up with new ideas)**

- Insisting is similar to making a demand. **(true)**

- Flexible people are very stubborn. **(false; they are willing to make changes)**

- Inviting someone into a group is a way of including that person. **(true)**

Answers for page 123: 1. D, 2. F, 3. A, 4. J

Review Words include • insist • creative • flexible

Fill in the bubble next to the correct answer.

1. Which word has about the same meaning as *creative*?

Ⓐ colorful

Ⓑ realistic

Ⓒ scientific

Ⓓ imaginative

2. Which word means the opposite of *flexible*?

Ⓕ stubborn

Ⓖ unfriendly

Ⓗ stingy

Ⓙ ugly

3. When you *include* someone in your club, you ____.

Ⓐ make him or her a club member

Ⓑ ask the other club members if that person may join

Ⓒ tell him or her that you are sorry, but the club is full

Ⓓ vote to keep that person out of your club

4. If you *insist* on going home, you ____.

Ⓕ beg the person in charge to let you go

Ⓖ politely ask the person in charge if you may go

Ⓗ wish you could go, but accept that you can't

Ⓙ demand to go home, no matter what

Writing

Write about something creative that you have done. Use **creative** in your sentence.

_____

_____

demolish

verb

If you **demolish** something, you knock it down or destroy it.

The builders had to **demolish** the old library so that they could build a new one.

Which of the following mean about the same as **demolish**?

- fix
- ruin
- build
- flatten
- tear down

What things in our town/city have been **demolished**? Was it on purpose or was it an accident?

deliberately

adverb

Something done on purpose is done **deliberately**.

Rupert **deliberately** turned up his music while I was reading just to bug me.

Which of the following are probably done **deliberately**?

- crashing into a pole
- tickling your sister
- pushing someone
- stepping on someone's foot
- bumping into someone on a bus

What has someone done **deliberately** to annoy you? How did you react?

coax

verb

When you use gentle words and actions to convince someone to do something, you **coax** him or her.

We used a dish of milk to **coax** the kitten down from the tree.

Which are examples of **coaxing**?

- Raul threw a temper tantrum when he couldn't get his way.
- Marta wanted to go home, but we talked her into staying for dinner.
- Sara sat quietly and held out a treat for the shy dog.
- "If you don't give it to me, I'll scream."
- Grandma spoke quietly and rocked the baby to get him to stop crying.

Tell about a time when you **coaxed** someone into doing something. What gentle words and ways did you use?

perspire

verb

When you **perspire**, you sweat.

After you do a lot of exercise and **perspire**, it's a good idea to drink some water.

Which of these might make a person **perspire**?

- running around a track
- lying in a hammock
- working in the sun
- playing baseball
- eating ice cream

What activities make you **perspire**? Why is it important to drink liquids when you are doing something that makes you **perspire**?

Review

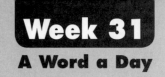

demolish • deliberately • coax • perspire

Write on the board the four words studied this week. Read the words with the class and briefly review their meanings. Then conduct the oral activities below.

❶ Tell students that you are going to give them a clue about one of the words for the week. They are to find the word that answers the clue.

- Many people do this while they exercise. **(perspire)**

- If you break something on purpose, you do it this way. **(deliberately)**

- The city was lucky that the earthquake did not do this to any buildings. **(demolish them)**

- If your friend felt grumpy and wouldn't come out of her room, you might have to do this. **(coax her to come out)**

❷ Read each sentence and ask students to supply the correct word to complete the sentence.

- I always ___ during my gymnastics workouts. **(perspire)**

- Please don't be mad. I bumped into you by accident, not ___. **(deliberately)**

- I hope they won't ___ that beautiful old building on Fourth Street. **(demolish)**

- I wish I could ___ my cat to sit on my lap more often. **(coax)**

❸ Read each sentence and ask students to tell which word or words are wrong. Then have them provide the correct word from the week's list.

- Let's command our sick cat to eat by offering her some tuna. **(command/coax)**

- My brother accidentally slurps his soup just to annoy me. **(accidentally/deliberately)**

- Workers used wrecking equipment to construct the old stadium. **(construct/demolish)**

- When it is very hot, our bodies hold water. **(hold water/perspire)**

❹ Read each sentence and ask students to decide if it is true or false. If the sentence is false, instruct students to explain why.

- Nervousness makes some people perspire. **(true)**

- It is rude to deliberately burp at the dinner table. **(true)**

- Bombs cannot demolish a city. **(false; bombs can destroy a city)**

- To coax is the same as to command. **(false; coaxing is gentle; commanding is firm)**

Answers for page 127: 1. C, 2. F, 3. B, 4. H

Name _____

demolish • deliberately • coax • perspire

Fill in the bubble next to the correct answer.

1. Which word has about the same meaning as *perspire*?
- Ⓐ shower
- Ⓑ bathe
- Ⓒ sweat
- Ⓓ drink

2. Which word means the opposite of *deliberately*?
- Ⓕ accidentally
- Ⓖ kindly
- Ⓗ angrily
- Ⓙ disrespectfully

3. Which sentence tells about *demolishing* a building?
- Ⓐ Architects designed a new high school building for our city.
- Ⓑ Workers tore down the 70-year-old building.
- Ⓒ It took builders about a year to finish the new building.
- Ⓓ Landscapers planted trees and bushes around the building.

4. You might *coax* a scared cat out from under the bed by ___.
- Ⓕ making fun of it
- Ⓖ ordering it to come out
- Ⓗ speaking softly to it
- Ⓙ threatening it with punishment

Writing

Write about what you'd say to coax a shy friend to go with you to a party. Use **coax** in your sentence.

_____

_____

ecstatic

adjective

If you're **ecstatic**, you are extremely happy and excited about something.

When our teacher said we were going to have a play day on Friday, the class became **ecstatic** and started cheering.

Which of the following mean about the same as **ecstatic**?

- sad
- thrilled
- delighted
- overjoyed
- unhappy

Tell about a time when you were absolutely **ecstatic** about something. How did that feel?
How is being **ecstatic** different from just being happy?

associate

verb

When we **associate**, we think of things that go together.

We **associate** hearts and flowers with Valentine's Day.

What is the first word you **associate** with each of the following?

- peanut butter and _____
- shoes and _____
- salt and _____
- bread and _____
- hide-and-_____

What is your favorite holiday? What are the things that you **associate** with that day?

category

noun

A **category** is a group of items that are similar in some way.

Apples, oranges, and kiwis are in the fruit **category**.

Name three items in each of the following **categories**:

- vehicles
- tools
- zoo animals
- buildings
- insects

Name several items you see in your classroom and tell the **category** they each belong in.

abundant

adjective

Something is **abundant** when you have a lot of it.

The farmer's corn crop was so **abundant** that his grain silo was filled to the top.

Which of the following describe an **abundant** amount?

- a 50-pound sack of rice
- a kernel of corn
- a hill of ants
- a sheet of paper
- a grain of sand

If you could have an **abundant** supply of something, what would it be?

ecstatic • associate • category • abundant

Write on the board the four words studied this week. Read the words with the class and briefly review their meanings. Then conduct the oral activities below.

1 Tell students that you are going to give them a clue about one of the words for the week. They are to find the word that answers the clue.

- If your refrigerator is full, this word describes your food supply. (**abundant**)

- Carrots, potatoes, onions, and corn fit into the vegetable one. (**category**)

- You would probably feel this way if one of your dreams came true. (**ecstatic**)

- People do this with pairs of things, such as night and day or dogs and cats. (**associate them**)

2 Read each sentence and ask students to supply the correct word to complete the sentence.

- I ____ the color red with Valentine's Day. (**associate**)

- The weeds in my lawn are so ____ that there isn't much room for grass. (**abundant**)

- I felt ____ when I won the spelling contest. (**ecstatic**)

- The nut ____ includes almonds, walnuts, and pecans. (**category**)

3 Read each sentence and ask students to tell which word is wrong. Then have them provide the correct word from the week's list.

- Candy is always scarce on Halloween. (**scarce/abundant**)

- Sophie feels miserable about winning a first-place medal. (**miserable/ecstatic**)

- Since we often eat peanut butter and jelly together, we separate the two in our minds. (**separate/associate**)

4 Read each sentence and ask students to decide if it is true or false. If the sentence is false, instruct students to explain why.

- A category is one item in a group. (**false; a category is the whole group of similar items**)

- Crops are more abundant when there is enough rain. (**true**)

- Many people associate the color green with nature. (**true**)

- Most people feel ecstatic when they are sick. (**false; most sick people do not feel excited and happy**)

Answers for page 131: 1. D, 2. H, 3. B, 4. G

Review Words   ecstatic • associate • category • abundant

Fill in the bubble next to the correct answer.

1. Which word has about the same meaning as *abundant*?
Ⓐ green
Ⓑ healthful
Ⓒ scarce
Ⓓ plentiful

2. Which word means the opposite of *ecstatic*?
Ⓕ interested
Ⓖ satisfied
Ⓗ miserable
Ⓙ joyful

3. Which sentence tells about a *category*?
Ⓐ Our family eats beef about once a month.
Ⓑ Tuna, salmon, and halibut are types of fish.
Ⓒ Dad makes a salad for dinner every evening.
Ⓓ Tapioca pudding is a delicious dessert.

4. Many people *associate* Thanksgiving with ____.
Ⓕ a legal holiday
Ⓖ pumpkins and turkeys
Ⓗ the last Thursday of the month
Ⓙ November 26 of last year

Writing

Write about a category of things you own. Use **category** in your sentence.

_____

_____

neglect

verb

When you do not take good care of something, you **neglect** it.

He **neglected** his plants all summer, so they died.

Which of these are OK to **neglect**?

- a pet
- a broken toy
- a paper flower
- your homework
- your friend's feelings

What is something that you've **neglected**? What happened as a result? What is something that you haven't **neglected**? What were the results?

pursue

verb

When you **pursue** something, you follow or chase it in an attempt to get it.

She is going to **pursue** her dream of being a doctor, no matter how long it takes.

Which of these are examples of **pursuing** something?

- a cat chasing a mouse
- a girl riding a bicycle
- a police officer running after a thief
- a student following his or her teacher's instructions
- a child following a ball that rolled away

What is a dream you want to **pursue** in the future?

abolish

verb

When you **abolish** something, you put an end to it.

I would like to **abolish** pollution.

Which words mean about the same as **abolish**?

- continue
- wipe out
- end
- save
- keep

If you could choose one thing to **abolish**, what would it be? Tell why.

feeble

adjective

Someone or something that is **feeble** is very weak or frail.

After recovering from a long illness, the **feeble** man had to walk with a cane.

Which of these describe someone or something **feeble**?

- a newly hatched baby bird
- an elderly person in a wheelchair
- a playful puppy
- an injured bunny
- a weight lifter

Have you ever felt **feeble**? What was it like? What can you do to help someone who is **feeble**?

neglect • pursue • abolish • feeble

Write on the board the four words studied this week. Read the words with the class and briefly review their meanings. Then conduct the oral activities below.

1 Tell students that you are going to give them a clue about one of the words for the week. They are to find the word that answers the clue.

- If we could do this to wars, the world would be more peaceful. (**abolish them**)

- A lion might do this to a zebra. (**pursue it**)

- When I did this to my lawn, the grass dried up and lots of weeds grew. (**neglected it**)

- This word describes an old woman who is too weak to walk very well. (**feeble**)

2 Read each sentence and ask students to supply the correct word to complete the sentence.

- Our principal wants to _____ gum chewing in the school. (**abolish**)

- I _____ to watch the time, so I missed the beginning of the movie. (**neglected**)

- A pack of wolves will _____ a sickly deer. (**pursue**)

- Grandpa is too _____ to climb stairs, so he takes the elevator. (**feeble**)

3 Read each sentence and ask students to tell which word or words are wrong. Then have them provide the correct word from the week's list.

- I took good care of my garden, so most of the plants died.
  (**took good care of/neglected**)

- Most dogs will run away from squirrels and rabbits. (**run away from/pursue**)

- Let's legalize air pollution! (**legalize/abolish**)

- My mom felt strong when she broke her ankle and had to use crutches. (**strong/feeble**)

4 Read each sentence and ask students to decide if it is true or false. If the sentence is false, instruct students to explain why.

- Illness and old age can cause people to grow feeble. (**true**)

- If someone neglected his or her house, it might need painting and repairs. (**true**)

- People can pursue dreams, goals, or careers. (**true**)

- Most people want to abolish politeness. (**false; most people do not want to get rid of politeness**)

Answers for page 135: 1. B, 2. H, 3. B, 4. F

Name _____

Fill in the bubble next to the correct answer.

1. Which word has about the same meaning as *feeble*?

Ⓐ hungry

Ⓑ weak

Ⓒ lonely

Ⓓ sad

2. Which word has about the same meaning as *pursue*?

Ⓕ ruin

Ⓖ hide

Ⓗ chase

Ⓙ welcome

3. Which sentence tells about an animal that someone *neglected*?

Ⓐ Last week, we took our dog to the vet for a checkup.

Ⓑ Our neighbor left her dog alone, and it howled all day.

Ⓒ Mom fed our cat Katrina first thing in the morning.

Ⓓ I brushed Katrina so her fur wouldn't get on the couch.

4. If we could *abolish* bullying, schools would be ____.

Ⓕ more peaceful

Ⓖ scarier places

Ⓗ full of bullies

Ⓙ prettier

Writing

Write about something you think your school should abolish. Use **abolish** in your sentence.

_____

_____

gallant

adjective

A **gallant** person is brave and fearless.

The **gallant** knight rescued the princess from the fire-breathing dragon.

Would a **gallant** person:

- run away if a friend was being bullied?
- lead the way through a dark forest?
- defend her sister if someone was saying unkind things about the sister?
- hide in the bushes when a neighbor came out to see who broke his window with a ball?
- go into a burning building to save a child?

Tell about a time when you or someone you know did something **gallant**.

milestone

noun

A **milestone** is an event of great importance.

The baby's first birthday was a **milestone** that was celebrated with a big party.

Which of these would be a **milestone**?

- taking a bath
- the first day of kindergarten
- going to the grocery store
- graduating from high school
- finding a cure for a serious disease

Tell about a **milestone** in your life. How did this **milestone** affect your life?

persevere

verb

You **persevere** when you keep trying and don't give up even if it's difficult.

The hikers felt like giving up after an hour, but they **persevered** and made it to the top of the mountain.

Which of these would you say if you plan to **persevere**?

- "Forget it; it's too hard."
- "I know I can do it!"
- "I can't go any farther."
- "I'll never give up, no matter how long it takes me."
- "I'll do it over and over until I get it right."

Tell about a time when you or someone you know thought something was really hard and almost gave up but **persevered**. How did it feel?

secluded

adjective

A **secluded** place is quiet and out of sight.

The pirates hid the treasure in the most **secluded** part of the island.

Which of these places are **secluded**?

- a city bus stop
- a single house high on a hilltop
- a cabin in the woods
- a grocery store
- an airport

If you could create your own **secluded** place, where would it be and what would you do there? What can you do to have **secluded** time to yourself even in your own house?

gallant • milestone • persevere • secluded

Write on the board the four words studied this week. Read the words with the class and briefly review their meanings. Then conduct the oral activities below.

1 Tell students that you are going to give them a clue about one of the words for the week. They are to find the word that answers the clue.

- Your high school graduation is one. **(a milestone)**

- This word describes a place far away from other people. **(secluded)**

- If you do this, you will probably reach your goals. **(persevere)**

- This word describes a person who protects and defends others. **(gallant)**

2 Read each sentence and ask students to supply the correct word to complete the sentence.

- Starting middle school will be a ___ in Amy's life. **(milestone)**

- I know this isn't an easy project, but let's ___. We'll be proud when it's done. **(persevere)**

- Mr. Green lives in a ___ spot with no neighbors close by. **(secluded)**

- The ___ dog rescued her human family from a fire in their home. **(gallant)**

3 Read each sentence and ask students to tell which word or words are wrong. Then have them provide the correct word from the week's list.

- If you stop trying, you'll reach your goal someday. **(stop trying/persevere)**

- The hermit lived in a crowded spot where he could be alone. **(crowded/secluded)**

- A cowardly firefighter rescued the kitten from a branch high in a tree. **(cowardly/gallant)**

4 Read each sentence and ask students to decide if it is true or false. If the sentence is false, instruct students to explain why.

- It is a milestone when a child takes her first steps. **(true)**

- Gallant people are selfish and fearful. **(false; gallant people are helpful and brave)**

- A secluded house might be surrounded by trees. **(true)**

- Usually it is harder to persevere than to give up. **(true)**

Answers for page 139: 1. D, 2. J, 3. B, 4. F

Name _____

Review Words   gallant • milestone • persevere • secluded

Fill in the bubble next to the correct answer.

1. Which word has about the same meaning as *secluded*?

Ⓐ fancy

Ⓑ beautiful

Ⓒ public

Ⓓ private

2. Which phrase means the opposite of *persevere*?

Ⓕ get some help

Ⓖ continue on

Ⓗ try harder

Ⓙ give up

3. Which sentence is about a *milestone*?

Ⓐ Our family eats chicken at least once a week.

Ⓑ Last Saturday, we went to my cousin's wedding.

Ⓒ Mom mows the lawn and weeds the garden.

Ⓓ On Wednesday, we will probably have a math quiz.

4. A *gallant* prince would not ____ .

Ⓕ leave someone who was in danger

Ⓖ marry a princess

Ⓗ dance at a royal ball

Ⓙ ride a horse that was too wild for most riders

Writing

Write about what you think the next milestone in your life will be. Use **milestone** in your sentence.

_____

_____

diminish

verb

If something **diminishes**, it becomes smaller or less.

Our food supply will **diminish** if the blizzard continues and we can't get to the store.

Which of the following can **diminish**?

- an ice-cream cone as you eat it
- a person's size when he or she diets
- a light bulb when it's left on
- the water supply if it doesn't rain for a year
- a chair as you sit on it

If you could have something that would never **diminish**, what would it be?

dismal

adjective

Something **dismal** is dark and gloomy.

Our day at the beach turned **dismal** after the fog rolled in.

Which of these are **dismal**?

- rough seas under a stormy sky
- a picnic on a sunny, cloudless day
- a dark house on Halloween night
- an unlit underground tunnel
- a hot day at a carnival

How might you brighten up a **dismal** room?

essential

adjective

If something is **essential**, it's absolutely necessary.

Chocolate is one of the **essential** ingredients in brownies.

Which of the following are **essential**?

- breathing
- eating
- playing the trombone
- staying safe
- watching television

What is something **essential** that you do every day?
Why is it **essential**?

unanimous

adjective

When a decision is **unanimous**, everyone agrees with it.

Everyone in the class voted to go to the zoo, so the **unanimous** decision was approved by the teacher.

Which of the following are examples of **unanimous** decisions?

- Everyone except Henry wanted to go.
- Talia won the election by a 10 to 0 vote.
- The entire school voted to have a carnival.
- The whole team wanted to practice for another hour.
- Jim went to the beach, but Marisela and I stayed home.

Think about a time when you participated in making a **unanimous** decision. What was being decided?
Was it easy to get everyone to agree?

Review

diminish • dismal • essential • unanimous

Write on the board the four words studied this week. Read the words with the class and briefly review their meanings. Then conduct the oral activities below.

1 Tell students that you are going to give them a clue about one of the words for the week. They are to find the word that answers the clue.

- This word describes a dark, rainy day. (**dismal**)

- If everyone votes for the same person, this word describes that vote. (**unanimous**)

- Ice cubes do this as they melt. (**diminish**)

- This word describes something that you cannot do without, such as food. (**essential**)

2 Read each sentence and ask students to supply the correct word to complete the sentence.

- To stay healthy, getting enough sleep is ____. (**essential**)

- The darkness will ____ as the sun rises. (**diminish**)

- I read a story in which a monster lived in an old, dark, ____ stone castle on a mountaintop. (**dismal**)

- It's ____: everyone wants chicken for dinner. (**unanimous**)

3 Read each sentence and ask students to tell which word is wrong. Then have them provide the correct word from the week's list.

- Dough and cheese are unnecessary pizza ingredients. (**unnecessary/essential**)

- Our hopes of winning the championship will increase if we lose more than one game. (**increase/diminish**)

- By individual agreement, "The Gallant Gladiators" will be our team name. (**individual/unanimous**)

- The cheery waiting room at the doctor's office made me feel even sicker. (**cheery/dismal**)

4 Read each sentence and ask students to decide if it is true or false. If the sentence is false, instruct students to explain why.

- We couldn't convince two people to agree, so the decision was unanimous. (**false; everyone must agree for a decision to be unanimous**)

- Pain from a broken arm will diminish as the arm heals. (**true**)

- Candy and soda are essential in a healthy diet. (**false; sugary foods are not necessary to a healthy diet**)

- Most people would like to stay indoors on a cold, dismal day. (**true**)

Answers for page 143: 1. D, 2. J, 3. A, 4. F

Name _____

Fill in the bubble next to the correct answer.

1. Which word has about the same meaning as *dismal*?

Ⓐ angry
Ⓑ bald
Ⓒ shiny
Ⓓ gloomy

2. Which word means the opposite of *essential*?

Ⓕ uncomfortable
Ⓖ fascinating
Ⓗ important
Ⓙ unnecessary

3. Which sentence tells about a *unanimous* decision?

Ⓐ We all agreed that Charlie would make a great team captain.
Ⓑ Some players like the park best, but others prefer the schoolyard.
Ⓒ After the game, some of us went over to Max's house for pizza.
Ⓓ Taylor wanted blue uniforms, but everyone else voted for red.

4. Sunlight usually begins to *diminish* ___.

Ⓕ in the late afternoon
Ⓖ at midnight
Ⓗ at 10:00 in the morning
Ⓙ at dawn

Writing

Write about what you think is essential to do well in school. Use **essential** in your sentence.

_____

_____

strenuous

adjective

A **strenuous** activity takes a lot of energy and effort.

After his **strenuous** exercise, the athlete needed to relax and drink some water.

Which of these activities would be **strenuous**?

- moving many boxes of heavy books
- picking up a pencil
- doing 100 sit-ups and push-ups
- jumping rope for 20 minutes without stopping
- opening a letter

Tell about a time when you did something **strenuous**. What was it? How did you feel? What did you do to rest afterward?

assume

verb

If you **assume**, you decide that something is true without asking or checking it.

I **assumed** it was okay to borrow my sister's shirt, but I was wrong.

Which of the following are examples of someone **assuming** something?

- I'm sure Dad will take us to the movies.
- I'll have a sandwich in my lunch bag.
- He won't mind if we use his bicycle.
- I'll always get an A on every paper.
- I'll never have a cold my whole life.

Tell about a time when you got into trouble because you **assumed** something that wasn't correct.

carpenter

noun

The job of a **carpenter** is to build things from wood.

My parents hired a **carpenter** to build some bookcases in my bedroom.

Which of the following might a **carpenter** do?

- build a desk
- build a house
- decorate a cake
- repair a barn door
- shampoo a carpet

Have you ever watched a **carpenter** work? What tools does a **carpenter** use? If you were a **carpenter**, what would you want to build and what tools would you use?

braggart

noun

A **braggart** is someone who talks a lot about how good he or she is.

The **braggart** couldn't stop showing off his prize and talking about how great he was.

Which of these would a **braggart** do?

- repeat the story of his success over and over
- put his trophy in a closet
- tell his friends that he's the best at everything
- tell the other team, "I hope you win next time."
- shout, "I won, I won, I won!"

Think about someone who acted like a **braggart**. How did you feel about his or her behavior?

strenuous • assume • carpenter • braggart

Write on the board the four words studied this week. Read the words with the class and briefly review their meanings. Then conduct the oral activities below.

1 Tell students that you are going to give them a clue about one of the words for the week. They are to find the word that answers the clue.

- This is someone who is always saying how great his or her stuff is. **(a braggart)**

- This is a worker who builds houses. **(a carpenter)**

- This word describes a long hike up a steep hill. **(strenuous)**

- You do this when you don't check to be sure that something is true. **(you assume)**

2 Read each sentence and ask students to supply the correct word to complete the sentence.

- Shelby hasn't phoned, but I ____ that she is coming to my party next weekend. **(assume)**

- Bicycling uphill is ____ exercise that exhausts me. **(strenuous)**

- Stop being such a ____! We've heard about your first-place finish five times already. **(braggart)**

- We needed new kitchen cabinets installed, so Mom called a ____. **(carpenter)**

3 Read each sentence and ask students to tell which word or words are wrong. Then have them provide the correct word from the week's list.

- Emily is a humble person who always talks about her good grades. **(humble person/braggart)**

- You can usually check to be sure that your best friend likes you. **(check to be sure/assume)**

- Our 15-mile bike ride was so relaxing that I was exhausted by the end. **(relaxing/strenuous)**

- We hired a plumber to build a new bedroom onto our house. **(plumber/carpenter)**

4 Read each sentence and ask students to decide if it is true or false. If the sentence is false, instruct students to explain why.

- A carpenter's job is repairing car engines. **(false; a carpenter's job is building from wood)**

- Most people enjoy being with braggarts. **(false; most people do not like being with those who brag)**

- You can assume that most third graders will be in grade 4 next year. **(true)**

- Lifting heavy weights is strenuous exercise. **(true)**

Answers for page 147: 1. B, 2. G, 3. C, 4. H

Name _____

Fill in the bubble next to the correct answer.

1. Which word has about the same meaning as *braggart*?

- Ⓐ sailor
- Ⓑ showoff
- Ⓒ coward
- Ⓓ hero

2. Which word means the opposite of *strenuous*?

- Ⓕ continuous
- Ⓖ restful
- Ⓗ boring
- Ⓙ upsetting

3. Which sentence tells about a *carpenter*?

- Ⓐ Mr. Marino fixed the pipes in our kitchen.
- Ⓑ Chris Kellett painted our living and dining rooms.
- Ⓒ David Lynch built a new closet in my bedroom.
- Ⓓ Jenny helped us plant a vegetable garden in our yard.

4. When you *assume* that you have enough money for lunch, you ____.

- Ⓕ check to see if you have enough
- Ⓖ ask your mom or dad for some money
- Ⓗ think you have enough, so you don't check
- Ⓙ realize that you don't have quite enough

Writing

Write about a strenuous activity you have taken part in. How did it make you feel? Use **strenuous** in your sentence.

_____

_____

Dictionary

A a

abolish • *verb*

When you abolish something, you put an end to it.

I would like to abolish pollution.

abundant • *adjective*

Something is abundant when you have a lot of it.

The farmer's corn crop was so abundant that his grain silo was filled to the top.

accurate • *adjective*

Something is accurate if it has no mistakes.

John was accurate in his spelling of all the words and got an A on his test.

adjustable • *adjective*

Something is adjustable if it can be changed to make it fit or work better.

An adjustable chair can go up or down to fit people of different heights.

admire • *verb*

If you respect and look up to someone, you admire him or her.

I admire people who can play a musical instrument.

advise • *verb*

When you advise someone, you give suggestions that will help him or her to make a decision.

Jamie advised me to buy the red shirt because it went better with my jacket.

ancestor • *noun*

An ancestor is a family member who lived long ago, even before your grandparents.

My mother's ancestors came from Spain, and my father's came from Russia.

ancient • *adjective*

If something is ancient, it is extremely old.

The king wore an ancient crown that had been handed down in his family for generations.

announce • *verb*

When you announce something, you make it known to the public.

The birth of my little sister was announced in our local paper.

annual • *adjective*

An annual event happens every year.

Our family gathers every June for the annual Chávez family reunion.

anticipate • *verb*

If you anticipate something, you expect it to happen and are prepared for it.

The weather forecast said to anticipate a storm, so we got our rain gear ready.

anxious • *adjective*

If you are anxious to do something, you are waiting eagerly for it to happen.

Kim was anxious for the circus to come to town because she loved to watch the trapeze artists.

applaud • *verb*

You applaud by clapping your hands to show that you liked something.

The crowd applauded when the firefighter brought the child out of the building.

appliance • *noun*

An appliance is a household machine that is used for a special purpose.

Our toaster is the oldest appliance in our kitchen. The microwave is the newest.

appropriate • *adjective*

When something is appropriate, it is right for that situation.

It's appropriate to wear nice clothing to a wedding.

ascend • *verb*

When you ascend, you go up.

The airplane took off and ascended through the clouds.

associate • *verb*

When we associate, we think of things that go together.

We associate hearts and flowers with Valentine's Day.

assume • *verb*

If you assume, you decide that something is true without asking or checking it.

I assumed it was okay to borrow my sister's shirt, but I was wrong.

astonish • *verb*

If you greatly surprise someone, you astonish them.

We were astonished when the magician pulled ten rabbits out of his hat.

Bb

babble • *verb*

When you babble, you make sounds that don't have any meaning.

When the baby started to babble, we knew it wouldn't be long before she'd say her first real words.

banquet • *noun*

A banquet is a big, formal meal for many people on a special occasion.

The chef prepared lots of food and a beautiful cake for the wedding banquet.

braggart • *noun*

A braggart is someone who talks a lot about how good he or she is.

The braggart couldn't stop showing off his prize and talking about how great he was.

browse • *verb*

You browse when you look at something in a casual way.

My mom didn't want to buy any books at the bookstore; she just wanted to browse.

Cc

canine • *noun*

An animal that belongs to the dog family is a canine.

It's not hard to see that dogs and wolves are both canines.

carpenter • *noun*

The job of a carpenter is to build things from wood.

My parents hired a carpenter to build some bookcases in my bedroom.

category • *noun*

A category is a group of items that are similar in some way.

Apples, oranges, and kiwis are in the fruit category.

cautious • *adjective*

When you're very careful and don't take any chances, you're being cautious.

We had to be cautious on the drive to school because there were many potholes.

characteristic • *noun*

A characteristic is a trait or a feature that someone or something has.

A long neck is one of the giraffe's most noticeable characteristics.

charity • *noun*

A charity is a group that collects money or things to help needy people.

The children gave some toys to a charity that sends them to sick children.

cherish • *verb*

When you cherish something, it is special to you and you treasure it.

My mother cherishes the tea set her mother gave her when she was a little girl.

coax • *verb*

When you use gentle words and actions to convince someone to do something, you coax him or her.

We used a dish of milk to coax the kitten down from the tree.

commence • *verb*

When you commence, you begin something.

When the players have finished warming up, the ballgame will commence.

conduct • *noun*

Your conduct is the way you act or behave.

The children's conduct at the assembly was so good that they were given extra recess time.

considerate • *adjective*

A considerate person is kind to others and thoughtful.

The considerate boy brought his mother tea when she was sick in bed.

content • *adjective*

When you are content, you are happy and satisfied.

The kitten was so content as she sat on my lap that she began to purr.

convenient • *adjective*

Something is convenient if it's useful, easy to use, and no trouble.

It's very convenient to heat food in a microwave because it's so fast.

cooperate • *verb*

When people work together to do a task, they cooperate.

If we all cooperate, we can clean up the classroom very quickly.

creative • *adjective*

A creative person uses his or her imagination to come up with new ideas.

My creative brother should be a writer, since he is always thinking up wild stories.

A Word a Day • EMC 2793 • © Evan-Moor Corp.

Dd

deliberately • *adverb*

Something done on purpose is done deliberately.

Rupert deliberately turned up his music while I was reading just to bug me.

demand • *verb*

You demand something when you ask firmly for it or order it to be done.

The teacher demanded to know who threw the paper airplane.

demolish • *verb*

If you demolish something, you knock it down or destroy it.

The builders had to demolish the old library so that they could build a new one.

destination • *noun*

The destination is the place where someone or something is going.

This year, the destination for our family vacation is Hawaii.

diminish • *verb*

If something diminishes, it becomes smaller or less.

Our food supply will diminish if the blizzard continues and we can't get to the store.

disaster • *noun*

A disaster is something that causes much damage or loss.

It was a disaster when the tornado destroyed all the buildings on the main street of town.

discourage • *verb*

You discourage someone if you try to get the person to not do something.

My dad discouraged us from climbing the tree because it was too high.

dismal • *adjective*

Something dismal is dark and gloomy.

Our day at the beach turned dismal after the fog rolled in.

disposable • *adjective*

Something is disposable if you can throw it away after using it.

It's better for the environment to clean up spills with cloth towels instead of disposable paper towels.

doze • *verb*

When you doze, you fall into a light sleep for a short time.

The movie was so boring that I started to doze off.

drought • *noun*

A drought is an unusually long period of dry weather.

After months of drought, all of the farmer's crops died.

Ee

ecstatic • *adjective*

If you're ecstatic, you are extremely happy and excited about something.

When our teacher said we were going to have a play day on Friday, the class became ecstatic and started cheering.

edible • *adjective*

Something that can be eaten is edible.

Rhubarb stalks are edible, but their leaves can be poisonous.

elderly • *adjective*

A person is elderly if he or she is quite old.

The elderly woman was 85 when she took her first airplane trip!

eliminate • *verb*

If you get rid of something, you eliminate it.

After we rake the leaves, we can eliminate that chore from our list.

encourage • *verb*

You encourage someone if you give praise and support to help the person believe in themselves.

Jill didn't think she could finish the race, but her coach encouraged her and she made it!

essential • *adjective*

If something is essential, it's absolutely necessary.

Chocolate is one of the essential ingredients in brownies.

expand • *verb*

When you expand something, you make it bigger.

You could see the flat tire expand as air was pumped in.

Ff

feeble • *adjective*

Someone or something that is feeble is very weak or frail.

After recovering from a long illness, the feeble man had to walk with a cane.

fiction • *noun*

Fiction is writing that tells about characters and events that are not real.

I wrote a story about a princess and a magic chicken for the fiction contest.

fidgety • *adjective*

Someone who is fidgety has trouble staying still.

The toddlers could sit still for only a few minutes before they got fidgety.

flexible • *adjective*

If you are flexible, you are willing and able to make changes.

Dad can pick us up after school because his schedule is flexible.

fragile • *adjective*

Something fragile is delicate and easily broken.

The fragile vase broke when it fell on the tile floor.

fragrance • *noun*

A fragrance is a sweet, pleasant smell.

As we walked through the rose garden, we enjoyed the fragrance of the many open blossoms.

function • *noun*

The purpose or job of something is its function.

The function of the microwave is to cook or heat food.

Gg

gallant • *adjective*

A gallant person is brave and fearless.

The gallant knight rescued the princess from the fire-breathing dragon.

Hh

hardship • *noun*

A hardship is a difficult situation.

The first settlers in America faced many hardships, including illness and hunger.

headquarters • *noun*

Headquarters is the main office where members of a group meet and decisions are made.

The police officer called headquarters to request help from more officers.

hesitate • *verb*

If you pause for a short time before you do something, you hesitate.

Bud hesitated a minute before jumping into the cold lake.

hubbub • *noun*

A hubbub is loud, confused noise.

The blue jays made such a hubbub outside my window that they woke me up.

Ii

impatient • *adjective*

An impatient person is always in a hurry and finds it hard to wait.

The impatient man left the bank because the line was too long.

include • *verb*

When you make something part of something else, you include it.

I plan to include all my classmates in my birthday celebration.

increase • *verb*

You increase something when you make or get more of it.

My dad said he'd increase my allowance if I started doing more chores.

independent • *adjective*

When you think and act for yourself, you're being independent.

My 90-year-old great-grandma is still independent. She lives alone and cooks and cleans for herself.

inflate • *verb*

If you fill something with air or gas, you inflate it.

The coach forgot to inflate the ball, so it was too flat to bounce.

insist • *verb*

You insist when you make a demand about something and won't change your mind.

Katie insisted on hiking in a dress even though her mother suggested she wear jeans.

instruct • *verb*

When you instruct, you teach something to someone.

My uncle is a lifeguard, so he can instruct me on pool safety.

irritable • *adjective*

An irritable person is grumpy and gets mad easily.

I get irritable when I'm tired and hungry. It's best to leave me alone when I'm like that!

Kk

knowledge • *noun*

Knowledge is what you know and what you learn.

My science teacher loves sharing her knowledge of nature with us.

Ll

landscape • *noun*

A landscape is a painting of natural outdoor scenery.

The art museum had a special exhibit of landscapes last spring.

launch • *verb*

When you set a vehicle in motion into the water or air, you launch it.

The space shuttle will launch into space next week if the weather is clear.

locate • *verb*

When you find something, you locate it.

I couldn't locate my favorite shirt, but then I found it in a basket of clean laundry.

Mm

mechanic • *noun*

A mechanic knows all about how machines work and can repair them.

When our car wouldn't start, we took it to a mechanic, who soon got it running again.

milestone • *noun*

A milestone is an event of great importance.

The baby's first birthday was a milestone that was celebrated with a big party.

mob • *noun*

A mob is a large, often disorderly crowd.

Police officers tried to control the mob that was waiting for the rock star to arrive.

motion • *noun*

Motion is any kind of movement.

The rocking motion of the ship made it hard to walk without falling.

mumble • *verb*

When you mumble, you don't speak clearly.

After the dentist numbed her mouth, Ariana could only mumble.

Nn

neglect • *verb*

When you do not take good care of something, you neglect it.

He neglected his plants all summer, so they died.

nonsense • *noun*

Nonsense is something silly that has little or no meaning.

It's nonsense to think you can fly if you jump high enough.

nourishment • *noun*

Nourishment is the food that a person, animal, or plant needs to stay healthy.

The newborn puppies got their nourishment from their mother's milk.

Oo

observe • *verb*

You observe something when you watch or study it carefully.

An astronomer observes the stars to learn new information about them.

opponent • *noun*

An opponent is someone who is trying to beat you in a contest or an election.

Sue's opponent in the tennis match scored the last point and won the trophy.

opportunity • *noun*

An opportunity is a chance to do something.

My dad has the opportunity to get a great new job, so we might have to move.

optimistic • *adjective*

An optimistic person always believes that things will turn out well.

Even though Jay had a broken arm, he was optimistic that it would heal in time for baseball season.

orbit • *noun*

The path that the Earth or another planet travels around the sun is its orbit.

Scientists learn more about a planet by observing its orbit.

Pp

parched • *adjective*

You are parched if you are extremely hot and dry and need water.

We ran out of bottled water and were totally parched by the time we had driven across the desert.

peer • *noun*

A person who is in your age group is a peer.

Mario worked with a group of his peers to clean up the school garden.

persevere • *verb*

You persevere when you keep trying and don't give up even if it's difficult.

The hikers felt like giving up after an hour, but they persevered and made it to the top of the mountain.

perspire • *verb*

When you perspire, you sweat.

After you do a lot of exercise and perspire, it's a good idea to drink some water.

persuade • *verb*

You persuade someone when you give him or her reason to do as you say.

Janie persuaded me to choose fruit for dessert because it's healthier than cake.

pollution • noun
Pollution dirties the pure air, water, and land of our planet.

Electric and solar-powered cars are good for our planet because they don't create air pollution.

ponder • verb
You ponder something when you think about it carefully.

Scientists ponder the existence of life on other planets, but no one has proven it yet.

positive • adjective
You're positive about something when you are absolutely certain of it.

I'm positive I left my coat on the playground, because I took it off to swing on the bars.

possession • noun
Something that belongs to you is your possession.

I keep my possessions on my side of the room, and my sister keeps hers on her side.

postpone • verb
When you postpone something, you put it off until later.

We had to postpone the picnic until next weekend because of the rain.

praise • noun
Words that express approval or admiration are praise.

The teacher was full of praise for her class because of their great singing performance at the school concert.

prepare • verb
You prepare when you get ready for something.

I studied my math problems to prepare for the test.

prompt • adjective
Someone who is prompt is always on time.

A prompt student is always in class when the bell rings.

pursue • verb
When you pursue something, you follow or chase it in an attempt to get it.

She is going to pursue her dream of being a doctor, no matter how long it takes.

Qq

qualify • verb
You qualify when you reach a level of skill or knowledge that allows you to do something.

Our team had to win three games in order to qualify to go to the finals.

quarrel • verb
If you quarrel with someone, you argue with words.

My brother and I usually get along, but sometimes we quarrel over our chores.

quench • verb
When you quench your thirst, you drink until you are no longer thirsty.

On a hot summer's day, there's nothing like ice-cold lemonade to quench my thirst.

 A Word a Day • EMC 2793 • © Evan-Moor Corp.

Rr

rapid • *adjective*

Something that's very fast is rapid.

My heartbeat became very rapid after I ran a mile.

reasonable • *adjective*

Something that is fair and makes sense is reasonable.

The produce prices at the farmers' market are more reasonable than supermarket prices.

recreation • *noun*

Activities that people do in their free time are called recreation.

For recreation, my dad likes to play tennis on his days off work.

request • *verb*

When you request something, you ask for it politely.

Margo called the radio station to request that they play her favorite song, and they did!

reserve • *verb*

If you arrange to have something held so that you may use it at a later time, you reserve it.

We will call the restaurant to reserve a table for dinner tonight.

respond • *verb*

When you answer or reply, you respond.

The invitation said to respond by phone if you planned to attend the party.

restrain • *verb*

When you prevent someone from doing something, you restrain him or her.

Joe had to restrain his dog so it wouldn't take off and chase the neighbor's cat.

route • *noun*

The path you take to get somewhere is the route.

The road was blocked, so we had to take another route to get to school.

Ss

satisfactory • *adjective*

Something that is good enough is satisfactory.

Her first book report was satisfactory, but the next one she wrote was outstanding.

scold • *verb*

When you scold someone, you tell the person in an angry way that he or she did something wrong.

The teacher had to scold her students for their rude behavior during the assembly.

secluded • *adjective*

A secluded place is quiet and out of sight.

The pirates hid the treasure in the most secluded part of the island.

significant • *adjective*

If something is significant, it has importance.

My mom writes about all the significant events in my life in my baby book: my first steps, my first loose tooth, my first day of school, and others.

similar • *adjective*

Two things are similar if they are very much alike.

My brother and I like similar sports, but the books we like are totally different.

solution • *noun*

A solution is the answer to a question or the explanation of a problem.

The detective found the solution to the mystery by studying the clues.

spectacular • *adjective*

Something that is unusually amazing is spectacular.

The glowing orange sunset was the most spectacular I'd ever seen.

statement • *noun*

You make a statement when you tell about or explain something.

Everyone waited for the president to make a statement about the peace agreement.

stoop • *verb*

You stoop when you squat down or bend over.

Natalie had to stoop to pick up the pencil that she dropped on the floor.

strenuous • *adjective*

A strenuous activity takes a lot of energy and effort.

After his strenuous exercise, the athlete needed to relax and drink some water.

strive • *verb*

When you strive, you make your best effort to do something.

I strive to walk a little farther every day on my morning walk.

struggle • *verb*

When you work hard at something that is difficult, you struggle.

I had to struggle to learn my spelling words, but now I never misspell them.

stubborn • *adjective*

If you are stubborn, you like to have things your way and do not like to give in or change.

The stubborn child refused to let go of the ball in the toy store.

surface • *noun*

The surface is the outer layer of something.

Before you paint a picture, cover the top of your desk with newspaper to keep the surface clean.

Tt

task • *noun*

A task is a small job or chore.

My sister's task every night is to set the table for dinner.

tattered • *adjective*

Something is tattered if it's old and torn.

Among the things in my great-grandma's trunk in the attic were some tattered clothes and antique jewelry.

A Word a Day • EMC 2793 • © Evan-Moor Corp.

theme • *noun*

A theme is the topic or subject of something.

Ana's party had a rainforest theme, so all the party favors were rainforest animal toys.

thorough • *adjective*

A thorough job is complete and leaves nothing out.

Grace did such a thorough job of cleaning that there wasn't a speck of dirt left.

transparent • *adjective*

Something is transparent if light goes through it and you can see through it.

We watched the fish at the aquarium through a large transparent window.

U u

unanimous • *adjective*

When a decision is unanimous, everyone agrees with it.

Everyone in the class voted to go to the zoo, so the unanimous decision was approved by the teacher.

unfortunate • *adjective*

Something that is unfortunate is unlucky.

It was unfortunate that Abby forgot to bring her swimsuit to the pool.

V v

vanish • *verb*

If you disappear suddenly, you vanish.

The moon vanished behind the clouds.

verdict • *noun*

A verdict is a decision made by a jury.

The twelve members of the jury discussed the case for hours before reaching a guilty verdict.

W w

withdraw • *verb*

When you withdraw something, you take it away or remove it.

I'm not allowed to withdraw money from my savings account at the bank. I can only add money to it.

Y y

youth • *noun*

You are a youth after childhood and before adulthood.

My grandpa delivered newspapers on his bicycle when he was a youth.

Z z

zest • *noun*

When you have zest, you show enjoyment and enthusiasm.

The clowns performed with such zest that the crowd got excited, too.

Index